Twenty-Something Ideas

The Thoughts, Beliefs & Behaviors

of True Success

For Mike.

Enjoy the book!

Randy Large

R L

ISBN-13:
978-0615749648 (True Success Skills)

ISBN-10:
061574964X

To Mom
with deepest gratitude

CONTENTS

ACKNOWLEDGMENTS

I have had many people who supported me on this journey, including Doyle Meyer, Dr. Nancy Shepherd, Marj Black & Dr. James Henderson, from San Juan College. Thanks for believing we could teach people a work ethic.
I would like to thank Rob Mitchell, Jennifer Miller and their staff (especially True Success Skills advocates April Mitchell, Heidi Sawyer, Su Hodgman, & Deanna Cooper) from the Meth Pilot Project (now AXIS/NEXUS) for allowing me to work with their organization.
I would also like to thank my friends David Berry, Bob Carr, George DiRe, Scott Eckstein, Mike Melancon, Jim Miller, Rob Mitchell, and Norm Tucker. All of the discussions we've had over the years have helped me more than you know.
Finally I'd like to thank Sherrie, Megan and Josh for the motivation to be the best person I can be. I love you all very much.

Introduction

How do you define true success? If you could wave a magic wand and become the best person you could imagine, what would that look like? This is the first question I ask when I begin my True Success Skills class at AXIS, a jail-based treatment program helping women overcome meth and other addictions, located in San Juan County, New Mexico. The question is straightforward, but often difficult to answer. They become so accustomed to how things are, that it is hard to see how they can be.

People caught up in the cycle of addiction have a narrowing of their field of view. "How things are" becomes a rut in thinking and behavior that is difficult to change. Behavior becomes automatic. When an addicted individual is triggered, he or she takes the drug and receives the reward. The reward reinforces the behavior, and the behavior is likely to continue. Once this routine is established, an automatic behavior is created.

We all have automatic behaviors. While most don't hijack the brain like drugs and alcohol do, they impact our lives just the same. What we think and what we believe can narrow our field of view. Our brain tries to automate as much thinking as possible so it can focus on threats. This evolutionary adaptation in our brain can get in the way of a truly successful life, however you define success.

Maintaining awareness of your thoughts and actions and how they influence the world, while simultaneously understanding what drives those thoughts and actions, is what I hope you are able to do after reading this book. Who you want to be is important to define (waving the magic wand), but understanding how you became you is equally important. For if you don't understand what is driving your behavior, how can you change it?

In the early 1990's, I developed a work-ethics curriculum with San Juan College. My experience in the business world had left me frustrated. It was becoming more and more difficult to find employees who had a strong work ethic. During a meeting with Doyle Meyer, the Director of Contract Training for the college, he mentioned that the owner of a chain of local convenience stores had asked for help in developing a training program that would reduce employee turnover.

The college was considering developing a mock convenience store, to teach potential employees how to run a register, stock the shelves, and run the gas pumps. I suggested the problem with turnover wasn't that employees were lacking the ability to learn how to operate a gas pump or a cash register, but an understanding of how important it was to show up on time, to get along with their co-workers, to do more than asked, or to be responsible. In short, they didn't have a work ethic.

After meeting several employers with Doyle, it became clear that the curriculum was sorely needed, and the Work Ethics Program was born.

I developed the curriculum, and the Department of Labor supplied the students. They sent us a group considered "hard to serve." They included people who had had more than a dozen jobs in the previous year, or who didn't want to go to college but couldn't get a job, or individuals with no work history at all. Many were long-term welfare recipients (some generationally). Many had a negative attitude, and those who could get a job couldn't keep it.

The four-week class was eight hours a day, five days a week. Lesson plans included commitment, responsibility, initiative, customer service, communication skills, respect, and many others. As I taught the lessons, I realized that this common sense information that had been so vital to my success wasn't as common as I thought. The reason these individuals didn't have a work ethic was that they simply didn't know. We discussed the ideas and put them into practice. As they began to see how the information could help them, they were transformed. They began to immediately apply the concepts to other aspects of their lives, not just the pursuit of a good job. It began to generate its own energy. They had hope. Many were so inspired that they landed jobs before the class was completed (although they insisted on finishing the program).

I thought about what had happened to create a generation lacking a work ethic. Why didn't they know? As I considered their lives and their stories, it became clear. A hundred years ago, many families lived on farms. They had to work to survive. They were often raised in extended families. They worked beside their aunts and uncles, grandparents, and most importantly, their parents. They learned a work ethic because they were exposed to it constantly. Today, children aren't exposed to work. They go to school, and their parents go to work. Children have little idea of what work is, and most aren't exposed to work until they become an adult. They aren't learning the vital skills they need to be successful, something that happened automatically a few generations ago.

When you look at the working poor, often the single parent is overwhelmed with just trying to keep food on the table. There is little time to develop a work ethic in their children, or a simple understanding of the relationship between individual effort and success, especially when the parent is working so hard, and so little is coming from it.

When welfare reform was initiated, San Juan College decided to take on the challenge of helping people transition from welfare to work. They used the Work Ethics Curriculum as a core component of the program and were very successful. A few years later, I began working with several local leaders to develop a strategy to address the growing problem of methamphetamine abuse in our community. The San Juan Safe Communities Initiative was the result of that effort. We brought together the business community, law enforcement, school administrators, judges, treatment providers, prevention specialists, community members, and those in recovery to develop a plan to confront the problem. I visited with treatment providers and addicts in treatment. Could the Work Ethics Curriculum help them as well?

I began to teach some classes for the addicts and alcoholics that were undergoing treatment. While they responded well, it became clear that there were deeper issues that were influencing their success. I began to modify the curriculum, and True Success Skills was born.

The ideas in this book are the fruit of that labor. I have not only taught these concepts to drug addicts and alcoholics, but to business owners, school administrators, political leaders, teachers and parents, front-line supervisors, and various organizational leaders. The ideas apply to all of us, whether you are running a multimillion-dollar organization, or trying to get along better with your spouse. Each chapter represents a unique idea, but they are all related. They are written in a simple, easy to understand format. While the ideas are simple, they are not easy. They will make you think. Some will challenge your beliefs about yourself and others. Some may make you uncomfortable. That's a good thing. Our desire for comfort is one of the greatest challenges to personal growth. To quote an English Proverb, "Smooth seas never made a skilled mariner." It is my hope that this book challenges you to become a "skilled mariner" in all that you do.

Responsibility

Imagine a pond with a surface as smooth as glass. If you threw a pebble into the water, ripples would move out in all directions to the end of the pond. It is amazing to consider that such a small pebble influences the entire body of water, but it does. The pebble has changed the pond.

Just like the pebble hitting the water, our actions influence every environment of which we are a part. Once we choose to enter an environment, we influence it. When you enter a room full of people, you change it. Some look at you and go back to whatever they were doing or saying. Some recognize you and say hello. Some see you and don't know who you are. However they react, people have been influenced by your presence. This is one of the principles of being human. There is no way to *not* influence it.

We have the power to influence every environment of which we are a part. What we choose to say or not say, what we choose to do or not do, is *how* we influence our environment. Whether we want to or not, our actions, our presence, just being, changes our world. With this awareness comes great responsibility. *That* we influence the world is a

1

fact. *How* we influence the world is a choice.

Human beings influence the world through relationship, and we influence relationships by what we *say* and *do*. On a larger scale, society is the result of what everyone in it says and does. Most people speak and act without much awareness of how their words and actions are influencing the world, but whether they are aware or not, influence is occurring. Imagine what the world would be like if we acted with full knowledge of how our words and actions were influencing others? What if we chose our words and actions carefully, so as not to do any harm? The world would be transformed!

This concept is the heart of responsibility. If we accept that everything we do is influencing our environment, we understand we are helping to create our reality. If we don't like our situation, making different choices and taking different actions will create different outcomes. We can use the power of our actions (what we say and do, or don't say and don't do) to change our world.

Our actions influence our relationships. For example, if someone you don't like is struggling with something, do you offer help? If you don't like this person, there is a reason. Not helping will keep things the same, or make them worse. Helping may make them better. Knowing this, why not help? If you are hanging on to resentment toward this person, your actions (not helping) are influencing the relationship. One small act has the potential to change things for the better, whether or not it is successful is not important; the fact that you offered to help is. That simple act of kindness not only has the potential to make the world better, it makes you better.

Think about all of the relationships in your life. Consider relationship as any other human being with whom you interact. The relationship may be as simple as saying "Hi" to someone in a checkout line at the grocery store, or as complex as the relationship with a family member that has existed all of your life. It is through these relationships that we influence the world, and it is through these relationships that we are influenced.

We interact with others without much awareness of how we are influencing them, and how they are influencing us, but influence is happening. When we choose to say hello to someone we meet, we are tossing a small pebble into the pond. When we choose not to say hello, we are tossing a small pebble into the pond. We *will* influence the environment, just like the pebble influences the pond.

Accepting responsibility for our life requires us to understand that everything we do is influencing our environment. While it can be an overwhelming thought, it can also be a very empowering thought. Now that you know you *will* influence every environment, you can choose *how* you will influence that environment. So, how will you influence your world today?

Exercise

Think about how you have influenced your environment. How have you influenced your relationships and how have they influenced you? Have you had a relationship that ended badly? How did your behavior impact the outcome? Is there a current relationship you would like to improve? How are you influencing that relationship? What actions could you take that would change the relationship in a positive way?

Make a commitment not to argue for a day. Then pay attention to how your change in behavior influences others' behavior. When they say something you disagree with, don't argue. Watch for how that affects them. They may conclude you are not arguing because you agree, but their beliefs aren't your responsibility. Your goal is to simply become aware of your influence.

Offer a compliment to someone you don't like. Find something worthy of your praise, and give it. Don't ask for acknowledgement or any kind of response. Just give the compliment and move on. Giving a compliment to someone we don't like is difficult to do. That is why you should do it. We have such an investment in not liking him or her, that it is difficult to change our belief. But our belief is driving our behavior, and our behavior is influencing our environment in a negative way. Change your behavior, and you change your environment.

Teach yourself to see how your actions influence your environment. Change them to create different outcomes. You have more power than you know.

Blame

When a branch falls from a tree, it does not blame the wind. When a gazelle loses offspring to a predator, it doesn't blame the lion. They are not capable of blame, but if they were, what purpose would it serve? Survival requires them to adapt; they must focus on the present. They don't dwell on the past. They thrive because of their ability to move forward. Blame is strictly human behavior. It focuses our energy on the past, away from the present, and away from responsibility.

Blame is the opposite of responsibility. If you blame someone else, or circumstances for your life, you are *not* accepting responsibility. You are responsible when you accept that you influence every environment of which you are a part, and understand that your choices affect your outcomes. When you do this, you create a responsible and empowered life. Responsibility means accepting that you influence *everything*. If you blame others, the natural conclusion is that there was nothing you could do then, and nothing you can do now, to change the situation; this belief denies responsibility.

Blame is easy. If someone is disrespectful to you and you respond with disrespect, you can blame your behavior on the other person. They made you do it. If it is someone else's fault, there was nothing you could do; you don't have to change. The truth is, you made a choice. You didn't have to be disrespectful. By blaming others, you are implying that they control your response. This is why blame is so insidious. It promotes the idea of powerlessness. You couldn't control yourself. Your behavior was their fault!

We all have the power to choose how we respond; blame gives away that power. Responsibility is the awareness of your power. Being aware of it is the first step in learning to use power effectively.

Exercise

Whenever you hear blame coming from your mouth, use it to trigger your awareness. Why are you blaming? Ask yourself, "How did I contribute to this situation?" Blame serves no purpose other than to avoid responsibility. If you make a mistake, focus on the solution rather than blame.

If someone else makes a mistake, focus on immediate action to fix it, rather than who should be blamed. Don't ask for an excuse. That may lead to blame or justification. There will be time later to figure out how to prevent the problem from happening in the future. Accept responsibility for solving the problem now.

People use blame to justify their actions. When they do, they want you to agree with them. If they can get someone else to say their actions were justified, it lets them off the hook. When someone is seeking validation for his or her action, proceed with caution. When you hear others placing blame, understand that they are moving in the wrong direction. Help them to focus on the solution, rather than blame. If they insist in looking backward rather than forward, ask them what role they played in the situation. This may move their thinking away from blame and toward responsibility.

Blame can prevent you from finding a solution. It is a rush to judgment. Rather than judge, try to focus on *what* happened, rather than *why* it happened. Sometimes, defining *what* happened without assigning blame is very helpful in finding a solution. *Why* requires judgment, *what* requires objective observation.

Blame is wasted energy invested in the wrong outcome. To accept responsibility for a solution doesn't mean the problem is your fault. It is a decision to focus your energy and attention away from blame and onto solving the problem. Deal with "what is" rather than "what should have been."

Relationship as Mirror

In the story of Snow White, the queen asked the magic mirror, "Mirror, mirror, on the wall. Who is the fairest of them all?" She wanted validation of her beauty. She wanted the mirror to tell her she was the most beautiful woman in the kingdom. She knew the mirror had to tell her the truth.

Our relationships are our magic mirror. They show us who we are, not by how others treat us, but by how we respond to how others treat us. We are what we do. How you treat people and react to how others treat you is a reflection of who you are. Treating others well or badly says a lot about you. However, it is only helpful if you are willing to see and hear what the mirror is telling you.

Before you act, everything is theory. If there is not a person to be kind to, how do you know you are kind? If there is no one to test your patience, how do you know you are patient? You may believe you are kind and patient, but until you have the chance to do it, you don't know. Relationships provide that opportunity.

Have you ever done something and wondered why? Did you have an unusual reaction to something someone said or did? If so, why did you react the way you did? Sometimes, our actions reveal things about us we are unaware of. If we learn to see our actions without blame or judgment, we learn who we are.

We form a mental image of ourselves based on our experiences, thoughts, and feelings. That image may or may not be accurate. Until we act, we can't be sure. When we interact with another human being, our actions reveal our true selves. If we do kind things, we are kind. If we do mean things, we are mean. What we do is the most honest part of who we are.

Our most difficult relationships are our best mirrors. If someone can say or do something that causes us to act in a way we don't want to, it tells us something about ourselves. If you believe you are a respectful person, and you react to someone with disrespect, what does that say about you? Is what you believe about yourself the truth? Or, is how you act the truth?

Let's take an example. A co-worker tells you, "Looks like you screwed up again." You respond with anger saying, "I didn't see you jumping in to solve the problem!" Look objectively at what happened. They say something. It triggers an emotional reaction in you. You react with disrespect. What they said was disrespectful. How you reacted didn't have to be.

Why did the behavior trigger a negative emotion in you? The problem isn't with what they said. It is with what they said *means*. They are saying it is your fault. They are reminding you that you've made mistakes in the past. They are implying you are not smart. All of these attacks are crammed into that short sentence. Because you felt you were being attacked, you became defensive. Why did you defend yourself by responding with disrespect? What can that teach you? What does it reveal about you?

Kind co-workers wouldn't push your buttons like that. They might say, "We've got a problem. How are we going to solve it?" After the problem is solved, they might discuss with you why it happened, and what you could do to avoid it in the future. However, that approach won't reveal your hidden insecurities. In a way, a person who can push your buttons is more valuable to you. Difficult relationships force us to see ourselves more clearly, if we are willing to see.

Your reactions can help you understand some of the feelings and beliefs that are lying just below the surface. You wouldn't have found them had you not responded with anger; and not had the courage to look at your behavior objectively. The difficult relationship provided that opportunity. I'm not suggesting you seek out difficult relationships. However, they can teach you a lot about yourself.

Relationship can also show us who we want to be. Let's say a friend introduces you to someone. How do you treat people when you first meet them? Are you respectful, polite, and attentive? We generally treat people well when we first meet them because we want to create a good first impression. We want people to like us. How you treat people when you first meet them shows you who you want to be. When you meet someone, you exhibit your best behavior. How you want to be perceived reveals what is important to you.

How you react to people when you first meet them can also reveal insecurities. Sometimes the desire to be liked is stronger than our desire to maintain our boundaries. If someone treats you in a way you don't like, and you don't say anything to them, that tells you something about yourself. If you didn't confront, that is information. Why didn't you say anything? That they triggered insecurity in you is information. You wouldn't have learned this about yourself had you not met the person. It is through the mirror of relationship that we truly discover who we are.

We are not just the person living in our head. We are a force that is influencing the world through our actions. When we understand ourselves, we are more capable of creating positive influence and less likely to do harm. Relationships teach us who we are because they are what instigate action. Our actions become our teacher.

Exercise

Can someone make you angry? You can't control how they make you feel, but you can control whether or not you act on those feelings. The next time someone makes you angry, don't show anger. Control your response. You will limit the damage you could cause by lashing out. Express how you feel, but express it without showing it. Tell the person that their behavior has made you very angry, but don't show anger.

If you respond to people based on how they make you feel, you are at their mercy. They are in control of your behavior. Feel the anger, but refuse to show it. Expressing the anger in a positive way demonstrates poise and self-control. It is likely to influence their future actions in a more positive way than responding with anger.

The confrontation may be as simple as saying, "What you just did felt disrespectful to me. Is that what you intended?" Our only options aren't getting angry or not saying anything. We don't want to appear overly sensitive or aggressive, and we don't want to be someone's doormat. By expressing how the other person's behavior affected us, and doing so without getting emotional, we maintain control of our response, and don't allow someone else to control our behavior. We are also clearly establishing boundaries. We are letting others know what we will and will not accept.

Because you have chosen to accept responsibility for your life, you are now more aware of how you influence your environment. You are unwilling to blame others for how you react, and see relationships as a great opportunity to reveal more about yourself *to* yourself. Seeing relationship as a mirror will give you countless opportunities to see who you really are, and to practice becoming the person you want to be.

Our Actions

Thoughts and feelings tend to dominate our lives. But other people don't experience our thoughts and feelings. They only experience our actions. One can make an assumption about how we are feeling, based upon our actions, but our actions speak for themselves. What you do is the truest reflection of who you are. It is through your actions that you influence the world. "What you do" is how the world experiences you. Your thoughts and feelings are important to you, but it is your actions that are important to the world.

It's easy to get them mixed up. We spend so much time with our thoughts and feelings; we expect others to know what we are thinking and feeling. When something is bothering you, you tend to think about it a lot; you give it your attention. When you make that kind of investment in a thought, it's easy to assume others know what you are thinking and feeling. But the thoughts and feelings occur between your ears. When you express your thoughts and feelings, they enter the world. Until then, they don't exist in the world; they only exist in you.

Most of us don't separate our actions from our thoughts and feelings. We think about something, the thought triggers our emotions, and we react. It is a seamless process. We are often not even aware of our thoughts when action occurs. I remember driving home from work after a particularly stressful day, when all of the sudden, I became aware that I was gripping the steering wheel very tightly. I eased up on the grip, and realized my entire body was tense. I had been thinking about problems at work, and those thoughts had triggered stress. My body's response to stress was to tighten up. The thought (problems at work) led to the feeling (stress), which led to the action (gripping the steering wheel and tensing up).

Most of our actions come from our thoughts and feelings. Knowing this helps us understand ourselves, and others better. When we act, it can reveal thoughts and feelings that are below our level of awareness. When you are puzzled by someone's behavior, ask yourself what they may be thinking or feeling that has made them act that way. Try not to judge the action, as that may initiate a defensive response. And don't assume what you think is the reason is accurate. It may not be. Just try to understand it. It may give you insight into what he or she believes. If you really want to know, you can always ask. However, not everyone knows why they do the things they do, and the person may feel compelled to find an explanation for the behavior that may not be true. However, the opposite may be true. Sometimes, people don't know why they did what they did until someone asks, and they have to explain it. It is through the explanation that they begin to understand the action!

We can use action to influence thoughts and feelings. We often put off doing something because it doesn't feel right. Consider the quote, "It is easier to act your way into a feeling, than to feel your way into an action." When I began exercising many years ago, I had difficulty getting up early in the morning to do it. I read somewhere that it is better to set a smaller goal when exercising. My goal was only to get out of bed and get dressed in my running clothes. Once I was out of bed and dressed, I would say, "Well, I'm dressed and ready. I might as well run." When you are lying in a warm bed, getting out of bed to run rarely feels like the right thing to do. When you are up, dressed and ready, it makes perfect sense. Rather than lie in bed, thinking about how warm and comfortable it was, I chose action. I chose to get up and get dressed. No thought was required, just action.

Thoughts can paralyze us. Sometimes, we need action to get us up and going. Smiling when you feel down can help you feel better. Acting confident when you are insecure can make you feel better. Doing something on your 'to do' list rather than thinking about it will make you feel better. Whenever you find yourself in a funk, action is the best remedy. When you feel 'stuck,' do something!

Action not only affects you, it affects your environment. What you *do* is what really matters to the world. This is why it is so important to act with intention, with the knowledge of how our actions are going to influence our environment. Conventional wisdom says you have to show how you feel. This is not true. While it is important to express how you feel, negative thoughts and feelings are better expressed in words than in actions. If someone's actions are bothering you, it is important to let them know how what they are doing is affecting you negatively. Expressing it in words leaves less room for misinterpretation. If you show irritation but don't explain it, they must try to interpret why you are acting the way you are. Their conclusions may or may not be accurate.

It's okay to feel one way and act another, especially when it comes to negative feelings. Why would you want to act on negative feelings when doing so could create harm? Our actions should be based upon who we want to be, and how we want to influence our environment. If our actions are determined by how we feel, then anyone who can trigger negative emotions in us is in control of our actions. I'm not suggesting you suppress your feelings. Suppress your actions. Acknowledge your feelings; recognize them and explain them; just choose not to act on them if doing so could create harm. Express negative feelings with words and positive feelings with action.

Exercise

Whenever someone triggers a negative emotion in you, try explaining how you feel. Don't try to justify your feelings, or blame them on the other person. Just say how the behavior is making you feel. It might be something as simple as, "What you just said hurt my feelings." Don't show any hurt feelings when you say it, just say it with as little emotion as possible. This practice takes the attention away from your limbic system (emotional center in the brain) and puts it in your frontal lobe (the part of your brain responsible for thought and speech). It also helps you practice defining how you feel, which is a valuable skill.

Respect

How people treat you is a reflection of them. How you treat others is a reflection of you. Our actions show who we are. They are usually a reflection of how we feel. Think of a time when you felt the best you've ever felt; the best day you've ever had. How did you express yourself that day? Chances are you shared how you felt with everyone to whom you came into contact. You wanted everyone to feel as good as you felt. That's what love does. It pours itself out of you and into the world. When we feel great, we want everyone to feel great.

When we don't feel so great, how other people feel is less important to us. People who treat others badly are usually experiencing negative feelings. Negative feelings reflect an inward focus. When we are focused on what we think and how we feel, it's hard to think about others. When we aren't thinking about ourselves, we give more energy and consideration to others.

When people treat us badly, we often wonder what we have done. You may ask yourself, "Was it something I said?" or "I wonder what I did to make them mad." While you have likely influenced the situation, how they decided to act was completely up to them. How someone treats you is a reflection of him or her.

There are two kinds of respect. The kind you *show* someone, and the kind you *feel* for someone. The kind you *feel* for someone is out of your control. It is determined by his or her behavior. They act in a way that engenders a feeling of respect in you. If they do what they say they will do, you feel respect for them. If they have integrity, you feel respect. This feeling is automatic. It is an emotional response to the actions of another that create a belief in your mind about him or her. Whenever you think about the person, it triggers feelings of respect.

The respect you *show* someone is a conscious decision about who you want to be. Treating someone with respect is within your control, and is a reflection of you. If you are a respectful person, you show everyone respect. You act in a respectful manner, regardless of how another person treats you, or how you feel. Simply put, the respect you *feel* for someone is out of your control; the respect you *show* someone is within your control.

The actions you choose show the world who you are. If you choose to be a respectful person, you will show respect when dealing with everyone, whether a minister or a homeless alcoholic sleeping in the park. You may not feel respect for the homeless person, but you show the person respect, because that is who you are. Whether people are rich or poor, kind or mean, humble or arrogant, how you treat them is a reflection of you, regardless of how they treat you.

Exercise

Think about what respect looks like. Make a commitment to demonstrate respect to everyone with whom you come into contact. Make it a point to practice respect, especially to those for whom you don't *feel* respect. Think of someone you don't like, and make it a point to treat that person respectfully. Don't show affection or validate his or her negative behaviors, but be respectful, regardless of how he or she treats you. If you can do it with people you don't like, imagine how easy it will be with everyone else. The more you practice, the better you will become.

Also keep in mind what disrespect looks like. Make a commitment to avoid all disrespectful behaviors. If you act with disrespect, take a moment afterward and try to understand what you were feeling at the time that triggered that behavior. Identify the fear that was driving your behavior so that it has less power to control you. This will also help you to understand others when they respond to you with disrespect.

Confronting Behavior

There are two kinds of behavior you can confront, your own and that of others. While they require different approaches, the goal is the same: awareness. To confront is to raise the awareness of how behavior is impacting the environment, whether that behavior is yours or someone else's. People often see all confrontation as a negative or aggressive act. It is not. It is simply making someone aware of how their behavior is affecting you, or raising your own awareness of how your behavior is affecting you or others.

When it comes to confronting others, many people react in an aggressive or passive way when they feel they have been treated unfairly. How did you react the last time you felt unjustly criticized? Did you remain silent (passive) even though you felt hurt? Did you aggressively defend yourself? If you reacted in one of those two ways, how did it help to raise the awareness of the person who criticized you? If it didn't, his or her behavior is unlikely to change.

If you remain silent, how does that raise the awareness of the people who you feel have wronged you? If you don't say anything, how will they know? We have a responsibility to make people aware of how they are affecting us. Positive confrontation often leads to clarification, and a shared understanding.

If it bothers you, it is worth confronting. If you don't say anything, it will stay in your head. Once a hurt "sets up shop in your brain" it is likely to stay there. Every time you think about it, you relive the hurt. When you confront, you take it out of your head and put it in the head of the person whose behavior created the problem in the first place. That is the person in the best position to change their behavior to avoid the problem in the future. You want them thinking about how their behavior has affected you. Put it in their head. Confront.

How you confront is very important. If you respond by defending yourself aggressively, the other person is likely to conclude that you aren't listening, aren't being reasonable, or that you are defensive. A defensive reaction is likely to trigger an emotional response in the other person. Emotional responses don't usually lead to awareness, but to more hurt feelings.

If an emotional response leads to an argument, it is unlikely to lead to a positive outcome. Confront in a way that won't lead to an argument. Your goal is to make the other person aware of how his or her behavior made you feel. How can someone argue with that? Your feelings are your own. As long as you don't accuse the others of intent, how can they argue that you don't feel what you feel? For example, say, "What you just said hurt my feelings," rather than, "Why are you always trying to make me feel bad about myself?" The first explains how it affected you. The other implies intent. If you say how the behavior affected you, the other person can't rightly say, "No it didn't!" They can say they didn't mean to hurt your feelings, but they can't argue that your feelings were hurt. Only you know how you feel. Remember, the goal is to make others aware of how their behavior is affecting you.

When it comes to confronting your own behavior, asking yourself why you acted the way you did is a valuable question. When confronting others, it is important to make them aware of *what* they did, the *why* is up to them to figure out. You ask yourself why because you want to understand your behavior, and thereby understand yourself better. When you understand your reactions and the fears and motivations they represent, they are less likely to influence your behavior in the future. Once you are aware of them, it takes away their power to mindlessly drive your behavior. Awareness leads to mindfulness.

To change or influence behavior, you must confront it. Raising awareness (your own and others) of how behavior is influencing your environment is the limit of your power. Arguing, aggressive action, and manipulation are all attempts to control others' behavior. The most you can effectively hope for is to influence that behavior. You can't take away another's power of choice. Love tries to make others aware, and accepts their choice in responding to that awareness. All the love in the world will not change a person who refuses to see. When they make a choice, love is willing to accept it and move forward.

Exercise

Think of something someone has done that is bothering you. When it happened, did you say anything? If you didn't, ask yourself the following question. If you would have said something, how would that have changed the situation? Would you be thinking about it right now? If you did say something, was your response controlled and appropriate? If you responded emotionally, did it raise the other person's awareness or did it make him or her defensive? If you responded differently, how would that have changed the situation?

The next time someone says or does something that bothers you in any way, say something. If someone criticizes you, say, "Ouch." If they ask why you said ouch, explain how their behavior hurt you. Don't ask for an apology. Don't ask for an explanation. Your goal is to make them aware. That is all. If they try to explain, don't argue with the explanation. Simply say, "I just wanted you to know how that affected me." Accept what they say without argument. This will put the thought squarely between the ears of the person who has done something that has affected you negatively.

Self-control

The only power we have complete control of is the power to choose how we react to what happens to us. We don't have the power to control our environment or to control others; we have the power to control ourselves. We can't even control how others make us feel, but we have the power to choose how we react to those feelings.

When you use self-control, people see you differently. They develop trust and respect for you. The ability to manage your emotions and act with integrity in every situation is a challenge to everyone. Those who can do it are strong. People sense that strength intuitively. When you exercise self-control, people see you as an authority figure because you have mastered one of the most difficult tasks in life, the ability to control yourself.

Our choice to respond to what happens to us occurs in an instant. The choices we make are how we influence others. If you say or do the wrong thing, something that harms another, you not only lose their trust and respect, you lose self-respect.

Authority and influence over others comes with great responsibility. Just ask any parent. The more authority you have over others, the more important self-control becomes. Saying or doing the wrong thing can have long-lasting effects on a person, especially a child. Because people see you as having more authority, they give more consideration to what you say. You have greater influence. You must give careful consideration to everything you say and do, because it can do great harm.

In the professional world, the most powerful people (those who have the greatest influence over others) tend to exercise the most self-control. These people accomplish things with others through the power of influence, rather than the power of position. I remember once having a meeting with the President of San Juan College. I was there to pitch the idea of developing the Work Ethic Curriculum. It was a unique approach that hadn't been tried before, and we were going to ask the president to support an untested idea. As my boss and I, along with the vice-president of the school walked to the meeting, we discussed the plan. I had ten minutes to explain the concept and answer any questions he might have.

After I was introduced, we sat down at a large table and I gave my pitch. During the presentation, the president sat still with both hands on the table. He nodded occasionally, but was very still. When the presentation was over, he asked a couple of questions, I answered them, and we left. As we were walking back to the office, the vice-president said he thought the meeting went very well. He said the president's body language was very positive. I was surprised. I recognize body language, but hadn't picked up on any signals. I thought perhaps the vice-president was noticing the lack of negative body language, and was interpreting that as a positive sign.

That's when I realized why so many in power exercise self-control. Everything they do is subject to interpretation or misinterpretation. The less they say and show the less there is to misinterpret. They understand the responsibility that comes with their position, and they are careful not to say or do the wrong thing. When making big decisions, they are often more controlled and pensive.

Another benefit of self-control is it is comforting to others. If they know you are carefully considering what you are saying, it makes them feel much more confident about you. Self-control requires thinking before you act. What do you think about? The main thought is the consequences of your actions. When you do, you make fewer mistakes and create fewer problems in your relationships.

Self-control increases influence. We are always trying to influence each other. For example, if friends don't like someone, they want you to agree with them that something is wrong with that person. They are trying to influence your belief, not for your sake, but for their own. They are seeking validation for how they think and feel. If you agree with them (without forming your own opinion based upon your knowledge of the person), they have influenced you.

If you refuse to form an opinion based upon their opinion, you are maintaining control of your beliefs. If they can't get you to mindlessly agree with them, you are demonstrating self-control. Listen to what they are saying. Acknowledge what they are saying. Just don't blindly agree with what they are saying. They may not like it, but they will respect it. Your opinions are your responsibility. To give that responsibility to others diminishes your power. If they can bypass your judgment and shape your beliefs, or can get you to react to a situation without thinking it through first, they are controlling your behavior. You will not be perceived as powerful if someone can control your beliefs and your behavior!

Even to react in opposition is a way of giving up control. When you realize someone else has been influencing your beliefs and behavior, the natural reaction is often to resist it aggressively. For example, if friends gossip to you about someone you know, rather than just agree, you tell them they are wrong and you defend the other person. You may not have strong feelings for the other person, but you defend him or her because you resent the attempt your friends are making to influence your beliefs. To resist is reactive, rather than acting with intention. Whether you are agreeing with the person, or aggressively resisting, they both represent reactive behavior. Neither demonstrates thought before action.

Exercise

When something happens that triggers an emotional response in us, self-control is hard. But it is precisely when we are being triggered that self-control is most important. Take a few seconds to respond. A few seconds can make a huge difference in how you influence your environment. Take those few moments to consider the consequences of your actions. Then do what you think is best.

Sometimes, just taking a few moments before you respond influences the outcome. While you are considering what you will say, the other person feels compelled to say more. This gives you more information upon which to base your response.

Self-control requires thought and considering the consequences of your actions. Taking a few moments to consider what, if any, action you will take will dramatically increase the influence you have over others. After all, if they can't control you, neither can anyone else. You have maintained your personal power through the power of self-control.

Ask rather than tell

Newton's third law of motion (paraphrased) is that every action has an opposite and equal reaction. People follow the same law. They resist force. When we *tell* someone to do something, we create resistance. Even a two year old doesn't like to be told what to do. There is a simple way to avoid creating that resistance: ask rather than tell. If there is a way to ask rather than tell, asking is almost always the more effective approach.

There are times when it makes sense to tell. If a child is running toward the street, aggressively telling makes sense. If a fire chief is directing firemen fighting a blaze, direct commands are best. But if time isn't critical, find a way to ask.

Asking is effective because it doesn't take away a person's power to choose. Telling a teenager to, "Clean your room!" is likely to create resistance. "What can we do to make this room presentable?" is much less likely to do so. Taking a moment to rephrase a command into a question is worth the time.

Consider the difference between, "Hand me that report!" and "Would you hand me that report please?" Or, "Stop saying that!" and "Do you know how saying that makes me feel?" Asking shows consideration for others, but it really benefits us. If we don't create resistance in the first place, our relationships are healthier. Asking shows that we care about how our words affect others, and it shows respect. Asking rather than telling is one of the most respectful behaviors you can demonstrate.

You may not be aware of how your style of communicating is affecting others. It's easy to see when dealing with a child or a teenager. They openly resist you. Imagine telling children outside playing to come into the house. They may drag their feet, or walk in as slowly as possible. This resistance is easy to see. When you tell adults to do something, they may say they forgot, take twice as long to do it, or some other form of passive aggressive behavior. *How* we make our requests influences how others respond. Taking the time to consider how we are communicating what we want can dramatically influence whether we achieve it.

Asking rather than telling also helps avoid most arguments. When people say something we disagree with, it is hard to avoid the temptation to tell them they are wrong. If we disagree with what they are saying, perhaps we are misinterpreting what is being said. Asking for clarification is less likely to create a defensive response and more likely to promote understanding. After all, once you understand their point of view, they are much more likely to listen to yours. For example, if someone says, "People just don't care." you might ask if they think that you don't care. Rather than saying they are wrong, asking can get them to reassess their previous statement. Asking promotes thought; telling promotes resistance. Which would you rather promote?

Exercise

Be aware of how you talk to people and how they respond. If you find people resist you, that is a good indicator that people feel you are using force. When this happens, ask yourself if there was a way to communicate what you want by asking rather than telling. How others react to you can provide you with valuable information. Changing how you interact with people will change the way they react to you.

You may find it difficult to begin. You may perceive asking rather than telling as weak behavior, especially if you are used to telling people what to do. Try it anyway. If you are about to tell someone to do something, you already know what you want. You don't have to worry about seeming indecisive. Ask for what you want.

Asking gives the other person the opportunity to freely give. Because asking doesn't create resistance, it allows the person you are asking to focus his or her energy on contributing rather than resisting.

What does it look like?

Being an effective communicator requires you to say exactly what you mean. If you can communicate in visible terms (what it looks like), people will understand what you are saying. Effective communication also requires you to understand others better. When you ask others to communicate in visible terms, you both come to a better understanding.

The way to achieve visible communication is to ask, "What does it look like?" When you communicate with others, communicate in a way that answers that question. When trying to understand others, ask questions that will lead them to describe what it looks like. Variations of the question include, "Can you give me an example?" or "How will you know when you see it? Describe what it will look like."

We all come from different backgrounds and have different life experiences. Where we grew up, our religion, our culture, affect the way we communicate. Because we live in such a diverse world, communication is difficult. It is easy to be misunderstood, and easy to misunderstand others. Learning how to improve your own communication, and that of others, can dramatically improve your relationships.

Effective communication is a skill like any other. The more you practice, the better you become. People feel uncomfortable asking for clarification when they don't understand what someone is trying to say. If you are willing to overcome that discomfort and ask, you not only understand what the other person is saying, you help him or her communicate better. When they say it again, using other words, it improves that person's ability to communicate. You have given them the opportunity to practice their communication skills.

We use a lot of cliché when we communicate. Cliché is a phrase that has meaning beyond the words being used. It allows us to say something without really saying it. For example, if your teenage daughter says, "Whatever!" she is saying that she disagrees with you, but isn't going to argue with you about it. If someone accuses you of not caring, what they are saying is that you aren't demonstrating behaviors that show them you are interested in what is happening.

Cliché is imbedded in our language. When people use cliché rather than the words that represent what they want to say, they diminish their ability to communicate clearly. It also influences the ability to think clearly. Our words are a reflection of our thoughts. If a cliché replaces our words, it can also replace our thoughts.

As an employer, it is critical that I clearly communicate my expectations. When I ask someone to do something, I let them know what I want done, how well I want it done, and by when I want it done. I describe it in terms of what it looks like. I then give them an opportunity to ask questions. It's very important that they know what I want. Making sure they understand is also my responsibility.

To get another to speak in visible terms, you'll have to ask questions. The conversation might go something like this:

Wife: I'd like you to help out around the house more.

Husband: What would you like me to do?

Wife: I want you to clean up after yourself.

Husband: What would that look like? What is bothering you the most?

Wife: You leave your clothes on the floor instead of putting them in the hamper.

Husband: Ok, I'll stop leaving my clothes on the floor. Anything else?

Wife: Doing the dishes every once in a while. I don't like coming home to a sink full of dishes.

Husband: How about when one of us cooks, the other does the dishes? Would that work?

Wife: And I'd like you to put your dishes in the dishwasher whenever you have a snack, instead of leaving them in the sink.

Husband: OK, I can do that.

If the husband didn't ask for clarification, he might not know what was bothering his wife the most. Because he asked for specifics, and she gave them, he knows what helping out around the house looks like. When you are trying to understand what another person wants, keep asking until the other person describes what the behavior looks like. That way, you have no doubt as to what they are trying to say. Terms like, "helping out" or "picking up after yourself" are vague. If you can describe them in visible terms, "picking up your clothes" or "cleaning the dishes" there is no room for misinterpretation. I'm not suggesting that this conversation will guarantee the husband will pick up his clothes and do the dishes, but at least there will be no doubt about what his wife wants.

When I consult with business owners or other organizational leaders, one of my first steps is to clearly identify their expectations. If they say their employees are unmotivated (cliché), I ask them what it would look like if the employees were motivated. They may respond by saying the employees would show they cared (cliché). I then ask them how employees show they care. The boss will usually describe the desired behaviors as coming in to work on time, doing more than asked, getting along with co-workers, etc.

It usually takes two follow-up questions to get someone to communicate in visible terms. Coming in on time is something you can see. Doing more than asked is something you can see. Getting along with co-workers is still somewhat vague, but you could ask for clarification of that cliché. You might ask, "What does getting along with co-workers look like?" The response might be, "They don't complain about each other to me." Or they might say, "They don't argue with each other." Once I know what it looks like, I can help them develop a plan to achieve the desired outcome.

I ask specific questions because I want the boss to be able to define what the specific behavior looks like. If you are a boss and are unable to define it, how will your employees know what to do? Once you define it, you can go about making it happen. Until you define it in visible terms, people will not know what you want.

One of our greatest sources of disappointment in others is when they fail to meet our expectations. We often don't communicate those expectations. We expect others to just know. Sometimes we are not sure ourselves what we want. By taking the extra step of defining our expectations in visible terms, we not only help others understand what we want, *we* understand what we want. For example, let's say you are in a relationship and you want your significant other to be more affectionate. What would that look like? Would he or she kiss you more? Hold your hand in public? Touch you every time he or she walked by you? Whisper, "I love you." more often?

Be prepared to define the visible behaviors that show affection. You can say they should know already, and that if you have to explain it, it ruins the romance. However, our conditioning often determines how we act in romantic relationships. If the person doesn't know what you want, and has not experienced it, how will they understand if you aren't willing to explain it? The act of explaining helps you both understand what you want. You may have only had a vague idea of what would make you feel better, but once you explain it, you know! Replace the phrase, "I'll know it when I see it" with "Here's what I want you to do."

Exercise

Asking 'what it looks like' requires practice. Look for opportunities to practice getting others to describe things in visible terms. If someone says, "That person was rude!" ask what the person did that was rude. When you ask someone to do something, describe what it will look like when they are done. For example, rather than tell a child to "clean his room," ask that he pick up all of the clothes on the floor, organize his closet, fold his clothes, make his bed, and dust all surfaces.

If you are a supervisor, and employees aren't performing up to your standards, define those standards for them. Let them know what it will look like when they demonstrate the specific behavior. For example, if they are coming in late, define the desired behavior as walking in the front door at least five minutes before they are scheduled to work. State what you want to see in visible terms, and ask them to repeat it so you know they understand your expectations. If they repeat it and it isn't exactly what you wanted, that is an opportunity for you to be clearer about what you want.

Even in situations when you think you know what the other person is saying, ask for clarification in visible terms. This will get you in the habit of communicating for meaning. It will also help you realize how many times you misinterpret what someone else says. When you ask for clarification, they may say something that is completely different than what you thought they meant.

Thought

Thought is one of the most powerful forces in the world. It is the beginning of almost everything. Look around you. If you are in a building, whether it be an office, a house, or a library, it began with a thought. Someone wanted a building, an architect designed it, a builder built it, a painter painted it, but it all began with a thought. The art on the walls began with a thought. The furniture began with a thought. Every business ever created began with a thought. Every philosophy began with a thought. Every nation, every government, every religion, all began with a thought. Thought is the beginning of everything ever created. Thought is a very powerful force.

Your thoughts have helped create your life. A thought repeated frequently enough becomes a belief. What you believe about yourself and the world has shaped the person you are. If you want to live a better life, it begins with thought.

Imagining how your life could be is the first step toward making it happen. What would a better life look like? If you could wave a magic wand and have the ideal life, describe it in detail. What kind of relationships would you have? How much money would you make? How would you spend your time? Imagining the ideal situation has benefits. Thought is energy. How you use it determines what you get. If you spend less time worrying (energy consuming) and more time imagining (energy creating), you are investing your energy wisely. You are taking the first step toward creating something new. It begins with thought.

One of the most valuable thoughts you can imagine is envisioning the kind of relationships you would like to have. Think about what kind of friends you want and what kind of friend you'd like to be. What would it look like? How would they treat you? How would you treat them? What behaviors could you demonstrate that would make you the kind of friend you would like to be? What behaviors would they demonstrate to be the kind of friends you'd like to have?

If you find it hard to define what you'd like to see, define what you don't want to see. Sometimes it is easier to describe what you don't want, then define the opposite of those behaviors. For example, if you don't want someone to lie to you, then an honest friend is what you are looking for. An honest person tells the truth, a dishonest person lies. If a person lies, even though they may justify their behavior, it is an indication of how important honesty is to him or her. If honesty is important to you, you should seek relationships with people who share that value. People who value honesty understand trust is more important than any negative consequences of telling the truth.

If you don't like mean people, a kind friend is what you are looking for. What do meanness and kindness look like? A mean person says hurtful things, is critical of others or puts them down. Kind people don't say hurtful things, even when they are feeling hurt themselves. They don't criticize others, unless the criticism is constructive and is done in a way that does no harm.

Once you define the behavior you are looking for, and the behavior you are not, you can look for it in others. It is important to understand what you want, and what you don't want, before you look for it. Think about what you want. Imagine what it does and doesn't look like. Once you have thought it through, it is time to move from thought to action. Demonstrate it, and look for it in others. When you do, you attract the same behavior, and it all begins with thought.

Thought has a powerful influence on our lives, but most of it happens without a plan. You can use thought as the first step in creating the life you want. Imagine how you'd like the future to be (what it would look like), and then take action to achieve that reality. Everything begins with thought.

Exercise

Think about the type of person you want to be. What does that person look like? When you demonstrate those behaviors, you become that person. It begins with thought. Thought imagines what it will look like; action brings that person to life.

Let's look more closely at the example of kindness. What does it look like and what doesn't it look like? Kindness is expressing appreciation for others and what they do. It is listening when someone else is talking. It is showing affection, with a hug, a smile, a touch on the shoulder. It is showing others you are glad to see them.

The opposite of kindness is being critical, controlling or judgmental. For example, people who complain a lot and people who don't smile, or do not show consideration for others, etc. are not kind.

It is a good idea to avoid people who harm others in any way, whether or not they are aware of it. Look for people demonstrating kindness, and avoid people who do unkind things. Think about the kind of people you want to associate with. Look for people who demonstrate the behaviors you respect and appreciate. When you find them, make an effort to get to know them. Introduce yourself; ask them questions about themselves.

If you find yourself thinking negative thoughts like, "Why would they want to be my friend?" the answer should be self-evident. You are being the person you want to be, and that behavior attracts the people who find that behavior attractive. Kind, considerate people attract everyone, but especially people who are also kind and considerate.

Understand that thought is the beginning of everything you create. Because you influence every environment of which you are a part, you are always creating. Use thought to begin the process of creating the life you want to have.

Creative Thought

Two categories of thought are dramatically affecting your life: creative thoughts, and consuming thoughts. Creative thoughts involve imagination, understanding, and growth. Consuming thoughts involve worry, guilt, shame, and doubt. How your brain was formed when you were a child had a dramatic effect on the ratio of consuming to creative thoughts. Trauma, abuse and neglect can tip a brain toward consuming thoughts. Love, attention and nurturing can tip the brain toward creative thoughts. Your genetic disposition (nature) as well as your experiences in life (nurture), and how you responded to those experiences, have a profound affect on how your brain thinks.

When children grow up in a threatening environment, their energy is spent worrying. This can create a brain that is wired for consuming thought rather than creative thought. When children grow up in a safe environment, the absence of fear can create a brain that focuses more on creative thoughts. A brain that is wired to worry can also be very creative, but consuming thoughts can interfere with that creativity.

Your brain evolved to worry. Our ancestors spent most of their time struggling to survive. Their mental energy went toward finding food and shelter, and protection from threats to their survival. The people who could anticipate problems (worry) became our ancestors. Those who didn't worry did not survive. If you could anticipate problems, rather than simply react to them, you could do something to prepare for them in advance. Other animals have automatic survival mechanisms that drive their behavior, such as birds flying south in the winter, and squirrels storing food. However, those are instincts. Thought, while influenced by instinct, is different. The ability to think, and to worry, is what has allowed us to dominate Earth.

Once we achieved security, it was human nature to create. With a full stomach and a safe environment, humans began painting on walls, or carving figurines, making music, and enhancing their own beauty. However, creative thought was still a luxury. Most of the mental energy was spent worrying. There was a lot to worry about. Mother nature, war, wild animals, the safety and health of children were all threats their brains had to anticipate. They didn't have much time to relax and create.

Fast forward to the present. We all have brains that evolved to worry. We have all of this brainpower, and few threats to our survival that utilize it. Most of the threats to our survival are gone. Given that most of us don't have to worry where our next meal is coming from, or that barbarians are going to kick in the door at any moment, or that our children are likely to die from disease, our brain doesn't have to use most of its energy for survival. But the capacity is there.

So what does it do with all this excess capacity? It worries about other things. It worries about how we are perceived by others. Do they like me? It worries about our relationships. Is our spouse happy? It worries about our children. Are they safe? And in the absence of threats, it seeks them out by watching the news. Natural disasters, child abductions, financial collapse, and crime help the brain to do what it does best: worry. It is like a hyperactive child. Without a task on which to focus it's attention, it goes in all directions.

Because we are not focusing our thoughts, our brain goes where evolution and experience lead it. However, you can choose what you are going to think about. Worry is a thought. Doubt is a thought. Failure is a thought. You can't go to the store and buy a bag of worry, or a bag of failure. They only exist between your ears! You can consciously decide what you think about. If you think you spend too much time on consuming thoughts, practice imagination. Think about how things could be.

Exercise

The first step in changing your thoughts is to become aware of them. Sometimes, we become aware of consuming thoughts by the symptoms we show. Tension, depression, and moodiness, can all be the result of consuming thoughts. Any thoughts that make you uneasy over time can lead to dis-ease. When you become aware of these feelings, try to identify the thoughts that led to them. If you find that you have been worrying, ask yourself if those thoughts are justified, or if different thoughts would serve you better. I'm not asking you to ignore possible negative outcomes, just don't dwell on them. Acknowledge them, and then move on. Direct your thoughts elsewhere.

So what should you think about? It depends on the situation. If you need an emergency good thought, you can put your mind on a specific happy thought. If you are trying to improve your mood and confidence over time, a longer-term strategy of imagining positive outcomes is effective.

An "emergency good thought" can be something that completely changes your thinking. Imagine yourself winning $20 million in the lottery. Think about how you would spend the money. Imagine being debt free. Would you travel? Would you set up a fund to pay for any education your extended family would ever need? What would you buy first? Would you buy a new car? Would you buy a new house? How would you furnish the house? Would you quit your job or go back to school?

The goal of this mental exercise is to get you thinking something exciting and new, and change your thought patterns. If you were worried about some situation over which you had little control, thinking these positive thoughts not only changes your thought process, but changes your physiology as well. Just thinking these thoughts can make you feel better. Think with as much detail as your imagination will allow. Doing so uses mental energy toward creative thought, and takes it away from consuming thought.

If you are looking to improve your mood over time, imagine a better future. Set some goals and imagine achieving them. If your goal is to start a new business, imagine having that business. Imagine it being everything you expected and more. Is it a restaurant? If so, imagine greeting the guests as they finish their meal and asking them if everything is o.k. Imagine reading a positive review of your restaurant in the newspaper or online. You can then think backwards and imagine the steps you would take to make that dream a reality. What would you name the restaurant? What would be on the menu? Who would you talk with to secure financing? What would you include in the business plan? Whatever the goal, imagine achieving that goal and the steps you would take to make it a reality.

If you are looking for a successful romantic relationship, imagine what that would look like. Imagine dressing up and going out on a date to some special event. Imagine conversation over dinner at a fancy restaurant. Imagine snuggling on the couch and watching a movie you both love. Whatever the fantasy, imagine it happening. Try to envision it in as much detail as you can. Imagine where you might meet this person. Imagine what you would say when you first meet.

While daydreaming about your goals cannot make them come true, doing so changes your thinking. Knowing what you want to happen is the first step in making it happen. Imagination is the beginning of the process. This exercise will change your thinking from consuming thoughts to creative thoughts. Imagining future possibilities will put you on a different path, an exciting path!

Fear is the memory of pain

When it comes to experiencing pain, our brain's job is to respond and remember. The response stops the damage, and the memory is there to teach us to avoid the pain in the future. If a two-year-old girl reaches up and touches a hot pot on a stovetop, the immediate response to the pain is to pull her hand back quickly. Once the response has prevented further damage, a memory is created. The brain creates a clear, powerful memory of the experience.

She is much less likely to touch something on a hot stove in the future. The memory will be so strong it will become an automatic behavior. When her hand gets near anything radiating heat, the memory will be triggered and she will pull her hand back quickly.

The brain wants you to remember the pain, so you can avoid it in the future. This is why it is easy to forget a telephone number, but hard to forget a painful experience. The more powerful the memory, the more likely you are to avoid that situation in the future, thereby preventing harm.

The brain doesn't distinguish between physical pain and emotional pain. If it hurts, it creates a strong memory. This defense mechanism serves us well when it comes to physical pain. Pain serves a purpose. If we didn't have pain, we wouldn't stop doing the thing that was injuring us. Without the memory of the pain, we wouldn't learn to avoid hurting ourselves.

These memories actually become molecules. They change dendrites and synapses in our brain. The memory that is created is linked with other memories. Pathways are created in our mind, just like a path is created when we walk through a field of tall grass. The more we walk along the same path, the clearer that path becomes.

The more we think about a memory, the stronger the memory becomes. Since pain creates a stronger memory to begin with, we are much more likely to follow a painful thought and remember a painful memory. The more we think about it, the stronger it becomes. If we think about it enough, it becomes a rut. Anytime your mind gets near that rut, it is pulled in just like a wheel of a car is in a rut on the road. Once you are driving in the rut, it takes extra effort to get out of it. When you begin thinking in a rut, it takes extra effort to change your thinking.

When a thought is experienced enough times to create a rut, it becomes an automatic thought; it becomes a belief. Beliefs are very valuable. Fire burns, is a good belief to have. Sharp things can cut you, is a good belief to have. These beliefs and memories form a natural, healthy fear. This fear helps you become aware when dealing with fire and sharp objects or anything that causes physical injury. When you get burned enough times, you become afraid of hot things! That fear serves you well.

Let's review the process. Something painful happens. Our brain responds to the pain and creates a memory of it. The more painful the experience, the stronger the memory becomes.

When we remember the painful experience, fear is created. Fear is how our brain helps us to avoid painful experiences. Fear is the memory of pain. It is the mechanism our mind has created to help us avoid it. The fear influences our actions. If we are handling a sharp knife, we handle it carefully. When dealing with a hot pot on the stove, we use a potholder to protect our hands. Fear initiates protective action.

When someone says something that hurts your feelings, the same process occurs. We immediately respond to the hurt (although the response may not be as visible as a reaction to a cut or a burn), and our brain creates a memory of the pain. The more we think about it, the stronger the memory becomes. We develop a fear of it happening again, and take steps to protect ourselves.

We respond to emotional pain and the fear it generates by developing coping mechanisms. Most of our coping mechanisms are established in our childhood, when our brains are forming. Automatic responses to painful childhood experiences create pathways in our brains that can last a lifetime. If a child copes by ignoring the pain, he may become unaware as an adult. If a child copes by using outside influences to escape the pain, he may turn to drugs or alcohol as an adult. If what the child does diminishes the pain, the behavior is likely to continue. However, what works for the child may not work well for an adult.

People who have learned to ignore emotionally painful experiences can become unaware when someone is harming them and unaware when they are harming others. When I work with people overcoming addiction, they are almost always using drugs and alcohol as a response to emotional pain. One of the first things they must learn is how to deal with pain in a productive way, a way that acknowledges the pain, and doesn't seek to diminish awareness of it, or to avoid it at all cost.

All the walls we build to protect ourselves from emotional pain eventually become a prison. We can't protect ourselves from pain, only the awareness of it. Walls we build that protect us from the bad will also prevent us from experiencing the good. This is how our defenses become a prison. We cannot selectively choose which pain we are going to experience and which we are going to block from our awareness. Pain and pleasure are opposite sides of the same coin. You cannot have one without the other.

Exercise

Think about the walls you have built to protect yourself from pain. Are you guarded when meeting someone for the first time because strangers have taken advantage of you in the past? Are you defensive early on in a relationship because you don't want to get hurt? Do you compromise your boundaries because you feel any relationship is better than no relationship? Look at your behavior and seek to understand what is driving it. What thoughts or beliefs are influencing your actions?

Take a look at your reactions. How you react to others influences how you are perceived, and how you perceive

50

yourself. Reactions are a reflection of how you are feeling. Negative reactions are a response to pain or the memory of pain (fear). Ask yourself what you are afraid of. If you are trying to understand someone else's reaction, ask yourself what they are afraid of.

Defensive emotional reactions are a response to pain. It doesn't matter if the pain is real or perceived. If your behavior triggers the memory of pain in another (fear), they are likely to respond defensively. If you can train yourself to see the defensive responses of others as a response to pain, you can diminish your own defensive responses. Understanding someone is responding to pain usually triggers a compassionate response.

Focus your energy on understanding. This diminishes your own emotional reactions, and utilizes your thinking brain rather than your emotional brain. This allows you to act with intention, rather than just react. In doing so, you are much less likely to do harm, and more likely to have a positive influence on your environment and your relationships.

Belief

When you think a thought a pathway is created in your mind. That thought becomes a memory. Memory is matter; it is a group of cells in your brain. When you think a thought frequently enough, it becomes a belief. Once it becomes a belief, you don't question it. In fact, you seek to validate it. You look for proof that your belief is correct, and disregard evidence to the contrary.

Let's say that you meet someone and they say something that offends you in some way. The more you think about it, the more it bothers you. You dislike this person. You have formed a belief about him or her; you believe they are offensive. When you meet them again, you are less likely to look for their positive characteristics. You will seek to validate your belief about them. You listen carefully for anything they might say that is offensive. If they say something that could be interpreted positively or negatively, you are more likely to interpret it negatively.

It is hard to overcome beliefs. Once we create a pattern of thought that grows into a belief, our brain treats it like it is an investment that must be protected. How do we protect our beliefs? We do so by aggressively defending them and ignoring any evidence to the contrary. How passionately someone argues to defend a belief is an indication of how great their investment is in that belief.

So why do we feel the need to form beliefs? Our brain tries to automate our thinking for us. Anything the brain can automate gives it more time to focus on potential threats. It automates our thoughts to conserve resources. This is how you can drive into work with very little memory of the trip. You are deep in thought as the brain takes care of the driving for you. It is automatic. You don't have to think about it.

Belief makes our lives easier. It is easier to see something as black and white than to see shades of gray. Once we decide we understand someone or something, we can automate that thought process, and not give it much more thought.

This becomes a problem when we are dealing with something that is dynamic. It makes sense for our brain to automate tasks when we are dealing with something that is static (something that doesn't change), like a bike where the pedals and brake are always in the same place, or a car where the ignition, steering wheel, the brakes and gas are always in the same location.

Automatic thinking doesn't work well when dealing with people; people are dynamic. They are always changing. Every experience, every new thought, every new action, changes us. We aren't the exact person we were a year, or even a week ago. When our brain automates our interactions with people, it creates problems with our relationships.

53

When we meet someone, our brain creates an image of that person. It quickly makes a judgment. The first impression we have is often a lasting one. When we spend more time with someone, the image gets stronger. After a while, we experience less of the person through our senses, and more by interacting with our image of that person. If people stayed the same, this wouldn't be a problem. However, because people are always changing, our idea of them begins to diverge from the reality of them.

One area where this is easy to see is when a parent is dealing with a teenage child. Puberty is a time when a child goes through rapid change. It is often difficult for a parent to see the child as anything other than the small, helpless child that needed him or her to do almost everything. I once heard a mother of a high school aged child ask him if he'd like her to cut the meat on his plate! The image of the child is strongly imprinted on the brain of the mother or father. This makes it hard for them to see that the child is becoming an adult.

The more time you spend with people, the easier it is to interact with your image of them; you do not recognize how they are changing. If you think someone is immature, and you treat him or her as such, you are less likely to notice when they have matured. If you treat them as you would someone who is immature, they will resent you for it.

People change. See people for who they are, not who they were. Some people stay in unhealthy relationships because they are interacting with the image of who someone *was*, rather than who they *are*. We can err on the other side as well. We can have a negative image of someone, and fail to give them a chance because of who they were, rather than who they are. People learn, grow, and change. Treating people as if they haven't changed because it makes it easier for us, doesn't serve us well. It interferes with healthy relationships.

Exercise

See people. Study their faces. If you are in a relationship, look closely at your significant other's eyes. Notice the lines around the eyes and mouth. Try to see something that has changed in them. Look for subtle changes in how they look. Look for signs that their thinking has changed. Try to remember your first impression when you met them. How have they changed since then?

As a thought exercise, try to erase your memory of someone and see them with fresh eyes. There is no need to let them in on the exercise, just try to look without the memory of that person. It is very difficult to do, but doing so can help you to interact with the person in front of you, rather than the image of the person your brain has created.

Seeing Without Judging

There is value in seeing things for how they are. The truth can make you feel very good and it can make you feel very bad, but being able to see the truth has tremendous value. Lots of things can interfere with our ability to see it. Desire is the biggest obstacle. We may want something so bad that we refuse to see anything that contradicts the way we want things to be. When our belief tells us one thing, and evidence tells us another, we are conflicted. How we act in the context of that conflict shows us who we are. It takes a lot of courage to see things for how they are, especially when they conflict with how we want them to be. Sometimes we don't know what we want until we react (our reaction can tell us a lot about what we want).

Seeing the truth is also being able to see our reaction objectively and understand what it means. If we react strongly to a situation, it means we care. Have you ever heard someone yell, "I don't care!" at the top of his or her voice? The words say they don't care, but the tone says they do. Do you believe *what* they say, or do you believe *how* they say it? When in doubt, go with the *how*.

Strong emotions, both positive (love based) and negative (fear based) can prevent us from seeing things objectively. When we fall in love, our limbic system floods our brain with feel-good molecules, such as dopamine, serotonin and oxytocin. These molecules affect us by focusing our attention on the positive characteristics of someone and how those characteristics make us feel, and helping us ignore negative traits. Imagine how difficult relationships would be if the opposite occurred! How hard would it be to fall in love with someone if we only recognized all of the person's negative characteristics and were unable to see the positive?

Fear can override our natural tendency to love others. When loving someone has caused intense emotional pain, the memory of that pain can create fear that drives a person's behavior. People may look for any signs of negative traits and aggressively act to protect themselves should they see them. When this happens, fear has overridden the natural instinct to love. It not only interferes with healthy relationships, it can prevent them. While fear may help us avoid unhealthy relationships, if taken to the extreme, it can also prevent us from having healthy ones.

When we experience fear, our "freeze, fight or flight" instinct kicks in. Our blood pressure, respiration and heart rate increase. Our muscles tighten up as we prepare to run, fight, or freeze. This makes it difficult to concentrate. The more primitive part of our brain is trying to hijack our thinking brain. It is reacting this way because it perceives a threat. When we are experiencing a threat to our physical security, this response comes in handy. If we are experiencing a threat to our beliefs, it can prevent us from seeing what is happening in an objective way.

If someone does something that hurts your feelings, it triggers a negative emotional response. It can cause you to react, rather than act with forethought. How you perceive the interaction affects how you act in that situation. If you are unsure how you feel, your actions will tell you. If someone is disrespectful to you, it is a reflection of that person, not a reflection of you. There is no reason to defend yourself from the other person's belief. Their behavior is their choice, and outside of your control. If knowing that it's "their problem" and "not yours" isn't enough to prevent a negative reaction, consider this. If someone is treating you poorly, it is a reflection of how they are thinking and feeling.

You don't treat others poorly when you are secure, happy, and grateful. People treat others badly when they are sad, angry, or insecure. Behavior is a reflection of how a person is feeling. While it is not an excuse to treat someone badly, it is helpful to understand the feelings driving behavior. When someone is suffering, they deserve our compassion, not a negative reaction. Sometimes the compassionate thing is to say nothing. Other times it is to seek to understand how the person is feeling. Other times, it is important to make the person aware of how they are affecting you. The most important thing is to maintain control over your response. This is the only way to ensure you don't make the situation worse. This is the best way to avoid harm.

How others act is information. It can tell you a lot about them. How you act is information that can tell you a lot about yourself! You can learn to see behavior as information that you can use to understand yourself and others better. The key is to be able to see behavior objectively even though your emotions may be triggered. Focus on what is being said and done, rather than focusing on how it is making you feel. Seeing behavior as information is the best way to understand it.

When we judge the behavior of others, we often are seeking to validate our beliefs about the person or the behavior. It is a short cut our brain uses to try to make our life easier. Do the hard thing. Seek to understand rather than to judge. Use it as an opportunity to practice compassion, rather than defend your belief. You can't help but to form an opinion. The brain does this automatically. Continue to seek to understand what is happening. There is no need to excuse the behavior (judgment) or to criticize the behavior (judgment). Try to see the behavior in an objective way.

Exercise

Think about the last time you reacted emotionally to someone who "pushed your buttons." Your reaction is information. What can your reaction tell you about yourself? How about when someone responded negatively to something you said or did? What does that person's reaction tell you about them? Would you like those responses to be different in the future? If so, how? What would it look like? Rather than respond emotionally when someone pushes your buttons, make the decision to act differently. You could not say anything; give no response at all. You could give the person a hug. You could thank them, not giving any further clarification. Whatever you choose, choose how you will react now, and practice that behavior when the opportunity presents itself. See the response as information that will help you influence the situation to get a different outcome in the future.

Expectations

Buddha said that desire is the root of all suffering. When we want something, and are unable to let go of that desire, we suffer. It is natural to want things. When we don't get what we want, disappointment is inevitable. That is a normal, natural response. It becomes a problem when we are unable to let go of what we want when there is little or no chance of getting it.

Two-year-olds may throw a temper tantrum when you tell them they can't have something. The tantrum is their attempt to influence your behavior. Is the "no" worth the price they are going to make you pay? They are trying to increase your discomfort so they can get what they want. If they can get you to change your mind and you give them what they want, the response was worth it. If you hold your ground, they will quickly move on, giving up on what they want for the moment. They may cry for a couple of minutes (expressing their disappointment), but they will not do so for hours.

When we want something that is out of our control, and we don't get it, where is the line between healthy and unhealthy responses? Ask yourself if you can positively influence the situation to achieve the outcome you desire. If the answer is yes, then do it and hope for the best. If you can't positively influence the outcome, it is out of your hands.

If you can't change it, it is important to experience the disappointment. It is a healthy part of accepting that you cannot make it happen. The two-year-old tries to negatively influence the situation by throwing a temper tantrum. Part of being mature is being unwilling to negatively influence the situation to get what you want. If you have to manipulate and bully people into getting what you want, the value of what you receive is greatly diminished. Love is the way to receive. To receive something because of fear is the same as taking it. People of integrity are unwilling to compromise their principles to get what they want. They understand the way in which they achieve their desired outcome is more important that achieving it.

I'm not suggesting you give up easily. Making commitments and keeping them is one of the most important skills in living a successful life. The problem arises when we've done all we can, but keep trying the same thing hoping for a different outcome or compromise our principles to try to get what we want. If we compromise our principles, we will suffer. If we continue the same action without achieving our desired goal, we suffer.

Some suffering is good for you. It is part of the process of learning. As a child, you wanted to walk. When you fell, you suffered a temporary setback, but the suffering was teaching you how to improve.

It is a part of learning. The world provides lots of opportunities to suffer. We become unhealthy when our suffering greatly exceeds what nature intended, because we are unwilling to learn. Persistence doesn't always pay off. Sometimes, it simply extracts a greater and greater price. Our desire can blind us to the true cost we are paying.

It's easy to see this principle in action in unhealthy relationships (unless it is a relationship in which you are involved. Then it is hard to see). One partner may be holding on to the hope that the other partner will change. The other partner may say they want to change, but their behavior remains the same. They may profess their love, say they're going to change, and even show short-term improvement. When they revert to their previous behavior, their partner may use the short-term change as the justification to stay in the relationship. They *want* to believe. The desire becomes so strong that they are willing to compromise their boundaries and accept less than what they deserve. That approach will diminish them a bit every day, until they one day realize they don't know who they are or what they want.

Exercise

Define what you want. Say it out loud. If what you want depends on someone else, let them know. Once you have put your desire out there, it is up to the other person to do it or not. If they do it; there is no problem. If they don't do it, feel the disappointment. Don't get angry. Don't act out. Just experience the feeling, and see it for what it is. How important is it to you? Can you live without it and not be resentful? If it is something you feel you need, perhaps you must get it from another relationship. Does that mean changing or ending an existing relationship? These are questions you must be willing to ask.

Knowing what we want and being aware of our expectations can reduce our suffering. We will still suffer, but understanding why we are suffering, and being willing to let go of expectations can limit how long we suffer. We have more power than we think. While we have the power to control ourselves, our power with others is limited to influence. If someone is harming us, or themselves, it's difficult to accept that influence may not be enough to change their behavior. All of the love in the world can't save people from themselves.

Unmet Needs

Imagine you are walking through a desert. You have no food or water, and a thousand dollars in your pocket. After a day or two, you aren't sure you are going to survive. You are still 20 miles from the nearest town. At that moment, you meet a stranger who offers to sell you a gallon of water for 900 dollars. Fearing death, you give him the money and drink half the water immediately. He then offers to sell you another gallon of water for $50. What would you do? You have a half-gallon left, and only 20 miles to go. You may not buy the second gallon of water for $50, even though it is now only a fraction of what you were willing to pay a few minutes earlier. Why not? Because the need has been met. It is no longer motivating your behavior.

While dying of thirst is an extreme example of an unmet need, the principle applies to other needs as well. The need for approval, the need for acceptance, the need for attention, and the need for security are examples of potential unmet needs. When these needs are being met, they don't drive our behavior. However, when they are lacking, they can influence our behavior in negative ways. We are especially vulnerable when unmet needs are below our level of awareness. Sometimes you only become aware of the unmet need when you act. When this happens, it provides valuable insight.

When we act in ways that don't represent our best interests, there is often an unmet need driving our behavior. When someone buys a car that they can barely afford, what unmet need is driving behavior? When a young adult works 80 hours a week at a job to impress a boss who doesn't seem to notice his or her effort, what need is driving behavior? When a woman stays in an abusive relationship, what need is driving her behavior? When someone maintains a friendship, even though the friend is critical, self-centered, and mean, what unmet need is driving behavior? The answers to these questions vary with the person, but it is important to ask them if you want to understand what unmet needs are driving behavior.

Abuse or neglect, especially in childhood years, may create unmet needs. If they aren't met, they will affect adult behavior. I had a friend who pushed himself hard throughout high school. He took difficult classes, did hours of homework every day, and struggled to get the best grades he could. He did it all because he wanted his father's approval. His father never encouraged him or recognized his effort, and this made him want that approval even more. As an adult, his need for approval became unhealthy. If someone didn't give him approval, he would strive to get it, often taking time and attention from those who gave approval to him freely (friends and family).

It isn't just the past that can create unmet needs. Forces in the present can create them as well. The advertising industry is a primary example of negative influence. Part of advertising's objective is to create unmet needs within us. They want to motivate us to buy, by creating the impression that a product or service will make us sexier, happier, more liked, more respected, feel better, etc. Our value as human beings comes from what we do, not what we have. Advertising often tries to reverse that idea.

Exercise

When someone acts in a way that you don't understand, ask yourself what unmet need may be driving their behavior. The same applies to your own behavior. Asking this question can give you valuable insight into both yours and others' behavior. What should you do with that insight? If you can meet someone's need without any negative consequences, do it. If someone works hard on something, acknowledge the hard work. People want to feel valued. If a friend has earned your trust, tell them. People want to feel appreciated. If you agree with someone's opinion, tell them. People want to feel validated. As long as it doesn't conflict with your values, give people what they need.

Keep in mind that negative consequences can occur when we reward behavior we don't like. When someone is perceived as "needy" it is usually because they are willing to overstep your boundaries to get their needs met. People who insist you always agree with them, or who want all of your attention, or are unwilling to make a decision until you approve, are all examples of neediness. To give these people what they want can lead to more of the same behavior. Since your behavior influences every environment of which you are a part, consider the consequences of your actions before you act. Don't reward behavior that you don't want to continue.

Love and Fear

The root of behavior is love or fear. They are both valuable and important energies that direct our influence in the world. When you analyze all of your thoughts, feelings, and actions, they almost always come down to one of these two energies. Love's goal is to share, to grow, and to enhance. Fear's goal is to protect, to defend, and to take. Love leads to selflessness, fear to selfishness. Love gives energy; fear takes energy. Love increases your awareness of others; fear focuses your attention on yourself, taking it away from others. In many ways, they are opposites.

Fear pushes out love, and love pushes out fear. One does not exist where the other is active. When you look at the primary driver of action or behavior, it will likely come down to one of these two. You aren't one or the other, you are both; but your behavior only demonstrates one of them at a time.

We are hard-wired for fear. It is our brain's primary way of protecting us. Pain creates a powerful memory, that memory becomes fear. The memory of pain is an evolutionary adaptation. It is stronger because by avoiding things that cause us harm, we avoid future pain. The memory of pain is stronger, but it isn't necessarily a conscious memory. When we experience something positive or negative, a memory is created. The memory of pain is sent to an area of our brain that not only creates a memory in our conscious mind, but links that memory to our subconscious. While positive memories are more likely to be remembered consciously, painful memories are more likely to affect our subconscious. This leads to faster reaction times when we need to protect ourselves. However, the subconscious drive to protect ourselves interferes with a conscious, purposeful life.

Behaviors associated with love include compassion, kindness, patience, gratefulness, and affection. Behaviors associated with fear include aggressiveness, selfishness, criticism, condescending behavior, meanness, impatience, arrogance, and boasting. Many people think that someone who is insecure (living in fear) is a meek, passive person; someone who doesn't say much, avoids eye contact, looks down a lot, slouches, etc. But for many people, the best defense is a good offense. Their behavior is aggressive. When they demonstrate the behaviors associated with fear, they are showing you they are insecure. Attacking people is a sign of weakness, not strength. It is a sign of fear, not love.

Since fear is our "default response" it is easy to see how we can become more and more afraid with every painful event we experience. Our natural reaction is to try to protect ourselves from pain. How we protect ourselves is important. If we build walls, those walls may keep out the good and the bad. They will eventually become a prison if we don't let love in.

Let's say that a woman falls in love with a man. She is deeply committed, honest, open and giving to the relationship. After a while, she learns that he has been cheating on her. She finds that he has lied to her continually. She is shocked and overcome with grief. She feels humiliated. How could she have been such a fool? Why didn't she see the signs? The memory of this pain will create fear.

When her wounds have healed, and she is ready to enter into another romantic relationship, she may be overly sensitive to some of the signs she missed from the prior relationship. If he starts staying late at work, or canceling dates at the last minute, she may become suspicious. If she assumes he is interested in someone else, she may react as if it is true. Her reaction might be so strong that she drives him away, even though he isn't interested in anyone else.

Her fear has made her more sensitive to pain, and she is taking actions that she thinks will protect her from it. Her defensive reactions haven't protected her from anything. In fact, they have created more pain. They have also reinforced her defenses. When the relationship ends, if she doesn't accept responsibility for her role in the undoing of it, she may think she was right to accuse him of cheating. She created a problem in her mind, and acted as if the problem were real. Then she suffered the consequences of that action.

If she can't see the situation objectively, she may never learn how she is affecting her relationships. Every relationship needs the opportunity to succeed on its own merits. If we bring fear from previous relationships into the new relationship, it can negatively influence the new relationship to the point it cannot succeed. Pain and disappointment are inevitable in every relationship. It is how you respond to the pain and disappointment that determine how successful the relationship becomes. If you communicate through the pain, and build a shared understanding, you can resolve problems and build a greater foundation, the relationship becomes stronger. If you protect yourself from potential pain, and build walls, the relationship will weaken. You really can't protect yourself from emotional pain. It is part of life. If it didn't exist, neither would its opposite.

Exercise

When you demonstrate aggressive behavior, ask yourself what you are afraid of. If fear is driving your actions, there must be something there. The same applies to others as well. When you want to understand their fear-based behaviors, ask yourself what they are afraid of. This will focus your attention on their behavior, rather than how their behavior is making you feel. This response takes energy away from your emotional brain (your limbic system) and uses it to help your thinking brain (your prefrontal cortex) understand what is happening. Attention is going to be focused somewhere. Do you want to focus it on your emotional reaction or on understanding the other person? Wherever you choose to direct your energy, your attention and focus will follow.

We must choose to love in spite of fear. Loving action is never wasted. It makes the world better.

Walking wounded

Let's say you see a friend and pat him on the back or give him a hug, and he winces in pain. He was sunburned from a weekend at the lake. The pain you caused him wasn't intentional, and you quickly apologize. That's our natural reaction when we cause someone pain. We apologize and avoid anything that might cause more pain. You would be careful not to pat him on the back or give him a hug until the sunburn heals.

You can't always see sunburn. Clothes hide it. You find out about it when someone reacts to your touch. There are many wounds that are hidden. The world is full of emotionally sunburned people. You can't tell they are emotionally sunburned until you come into contact with them. Their reaction tells you they are hurting. We don't often notice because we react emotionally to their response, rather than seeing it with compassion, and understanding their response is a response to pain.

They are the walking wounded. They walk around, carrying their wounds with them, waiting to express the pain that is just below the surface. The slightest contact, and these people lash out in pain. They do a great deal of harm in the world.

To be fair, they were harmed as well. Their wounds were created from significant emotional pain. For many, the pain occurred in their childhood, when their brains were forming. The mechanisms they developed to cope with the pain, while an effective survival strategy at the time, now create more problems for them as adults.

People living in fear (the memory of pain) feel the need to protect themselves from threats, whether they are real or perceived. Because their pain is just below the surface, it is easy to trigger. When it is triggered, they respond aggressively. Aggressive behavior is a response to emotional pain. The response to pain creates more pain. It becomes a vicious cycle. If it isn't confronted, it can last for generations.

One measure of a person's emotional health is how past pain is affecting current behavior. Have they created defense mechanisms to protect themselves? Do they overreact to the slightest provocations? These are signs that someone is hurting. Just like the response when you touched your friend's sunburn, the defensive reaction is swift and automatic if you say or do something that triggers pain. The greater the pain, the less self-control a person may have. If they are hurting, they may lash out. When this happens, we usually don't respond intellectually because it triggers an emotional response in us. Their pain is creating more pain.

This is why it is so important to deal with emotional pain. If the wound isn't treated, it continues to do harm. It is like an infection that

73

grows, infecting other people. When the memory of pain is strong, fear is high. Fear focuses our attention on how we are feeling, and away from our actions, and the harm they can do. We become less aware. When fear is high, love is low; we are thinking of ourselves. When love is low, emotional health is low. Emotionally unhealthy people think of themselves and their pain to the exclusion of others. This is why selfish people are difficult to be in a relationship with. Their behavior is focused on how they feel, rather than how their behavior is influencing others.

Insecure people are afraid. Fear drives their behavior. Emotionally healthy people are kind and loving; love drives their behavior. It isn't the amount of pain you have suffered that determines your emotional health; it is how you respond to it.

Exercise

So how do you respond to someone when you trigger their emotional pain? Your response should be the same as if you had touched someone's sunburn. Apologize for causing the pain and avoid triggering it again. While the response seems simple, it's not easy. When someone responds aggressively to something you have said or done, it usually triggers an emotional reaction in you. Their response implies that you caused the pain intentionally, and you feel the need to defend yourself. Defending yourself is likely to escalate the situation. Use self-control and just apologize for causing pain. The other person may not even acknowledge being hurt. They may not understand that their aggressive response is a response to pain. Whatever the response is, your goal is to not make it worse. Do no harm.

Do no harm

There is both good and bad in the world. Most of it is the result of human behavior. When we influence our environment, we do so for better or worse. Our influence is rarely neutral. When we make a commitment to not making things worse, we make the world better. If everyone decided not to take any action that would make things worse, the world would be a truly different place. Making the commitment to 'do no harm' requires an awareness of the consequences of our actions, especially relating to how our behavior affects others.

Different situations require different action. If you use the transactional analysis model, you have three options when responding to others. Your response can be aggressive, assertive, or passive. In most situations, responding assertively does the least harm and has the potential to do the most good. If someone is aggressive toward you, if you respond aggressively, it escalates the situation. If you are passive, it teaches others that their aggressive behavior is okay. When you respond assertively, you confront the behavior without aggression. To be assertive, you must provide information without force. Your goal is to raise the other person's awareness.

Let's say you have a friend who tells you that you are stupid for making a decision he disagrees with. Telling you that you are stupid is an aggressive act. How will you respond to that aggression? If you respond aggressively, you might say something like, "It pales in comparison to some of the stupid things you have done!" This is likely to create a defensive (aggressive) response. What he said hurt your feelings. Your response is likely to hurt his feelings. A cycle of pain has started. To be fair, he started it. However, you have continued it. It could have stopped with you, but you reacted without thinking about the consequences of your action. Your action created more hurt in the world. It did harm.

You could have responded passively. You could have said nothing and just accepted the abusive statement. If you had, you would have taught him that it is okay to talk to you that way. While this response is less damaging than attacking him back, it also does harm. It has not made him aware of the harm he has done to you. He is likely to continue to speak to others that way as well. You have not made him aware of harmful behavior, and it is likely to continue.

Harmful behavior that you do not confront can diminish your own feelings of self-worth. It can create resentment. If you don't confront the harm he is doing, it will create a memory in your mind. The more you think about it, the stronger the memory will become. It will change how you feel about him and how you feel about yourself. It will also create fear. The memory of the pain has the potential to drive your future behavior.

The best way to improve the world is to do no harm. The best way to improve *your* world–your relationships–is to do no harm. We can't control the hurt others cause, but we can let the hurt stop with us. If we choose not to respond to a hurtful action with a hurtful reaction, we stop the cycle. If we respond assertively, and make the other aware of how their actions are affecting us, we chip away at the hurt that person may cause in the future. We are using self-control to influence our present and to shape the future in a powerful way. This is the ultimate use of human power, and it begins with the commitment to do no harm.

Exercise

When others say or do something that hurts you, you have the opportunity to make them aware of how hurtful their behavior is. Will you take that opportunity? Responding with aggression makes things worse. Being passive makes things worse. What should you do? Be assertive. You don't want to attack, but you don't want the behavior to happen again. The best approach is to make them aware. It could be as simple as saying, "What you just said hurt my feelings." How are they likely to respond? How they respond isn't as important as what you just did. You made them aware of how their behavior has affected you. Raising their awareness was your goal. How they respond is up to them. You should meet any negative response from them with an assertive response. If they are aggressive, tell them how that aggressive behavior is affecting you.

The conversation might go something like this:

Someone says, "You are stupid for making that choice!"

"What you just said hurt my feelings," is your reply.

"Am I just supposed to keep my mouth shut?"

"No. I value your opinion. If I didn't, calling me stupid wouldn't hurt my feelings."

"What do you expect me to do?"

"If you disagree with my choice, all you have to do is say so. You don't have to attack me by calling me stupid."

"I'm sorry. I was just frustrated."

"I understand that. Do you think that is a good enough reason to say such a hurtful thing to me?"

"No. I guess it isn't. I'm sorry."

This conversation and the resulting awareness wouldn't have happened had you not confronted the behavior in an assertive way. Every step of the conversation, you continue to focus on the goal: To make the other person aware of how his behavior is affecting you. It is a powerful response to aggression. Address the situation with self-control and poise. Don't show anger. Simply exercise the most powerful tool for changing behavior. Raise awareness of the harm someone is doing without doing more harm.

Your goal isn't to get the other person to agree with you. If you persist in trying to get others to admit they are wrong, you are using force. That force will create resistance. Your goal is to make the person aware. By confronting them assertively, you have done that, whether they agree with you or not. They may not even admit that you have made them aware, but you have. Have faith and confidence that your behavior has affected them. Awareness, once triggered, is difficult to suppress. They may justify their actions, or tell you that you are being too sensitive. Whatever their response, they are trying to avoid the consequences of their action. Gently bring them back to awareness. Confront all aggressive behavior with an assertive response. Keep your goal in mind. Don't use force. Don't try to get them to admit their error. Don't try to get them to agree with you. Simply make them aware of how their behavior has affected you. That is enough.

It is a simple process, but it is hard to do. Why? Because when someone is aggressive toward us, it triggers an emotional response. Our limbic system is flooding our body with the molecules required for fight or flight. Whenever someone is aggressive, our heart rate increases, our muscles tighten, our blood pressure rises. These things happen, regardless of what we choose to do. Regardless of how we feel, we have a choice in how we respond.

Shaping how we perceive the behavior can reduce the limbic system response. If we see aggressive behavior as being triggered from fear (which it ultimately is), we are less likely to become defensive ourselves. Fear comes from pain. We didn't cause it, we aren't responsible for it, but we can have compassion toward it. Compassion reduces the fight or flight response from our brain. It gives us time to think before we act.

By changing how we perceive the actions of others, by seeing it for what it is, we are able to limit our emotional response and control ourselves better. We can then act with intention, rather than simply reacting. This reduces the chance of doing harm. Self-control is hard, but it demonstrates the greatest strength a person can have.

Relationship

When you first meet someone, you know very little about him or her. You may notice how he dresses, or how she carries herself, and make assumptions about the type of person he or she is, but you don't know or understand that person. Relationship begins with communication, and it grows with understanding. When you understand the other person, and the other person understands you, you have a shared understanding. Relationship is shared understanding with another.

We are social beings, so we are naturally drawn to relationships. We want to know people, and we want them to know and like us. When you meet someone, you look for things you have in common with them. You ask them questions about themselves, and you tell them things you'd like them to know about you. We all try to put our best foot forward when meeting someone for the first time so they will have a positive first impression. In the beginning of relationship, we try hard to understand and to be understood.

In the beginning of relationships, your trust level is high. If an acquaintance says something that hurts your feelings, you assume it wasn't on purpose. You ask for clarification, they give it, and you understand what they meant. You misunderstood what they said, you now know what they meant, and your feelings aren't hurt. Because you confronted them by asking for clarification, you developed a greater shared understanding. If they ever say the same thing in the future, you won't be upset because you know what they mean by it. However, they may not say it in the future because they now know you are sensitive to it, and it might be better to simply avoid saying it.

The longer we are in a relationship with someone, the greater our shared understanding becomes. The relationship will strengthen as long as we are willing to work toward that greater understanding. Over time, you may be able to finish each other's sentences, or when something unusual happens, look at each other and know what the other person is thinking. Knowing there is someone who understands you and cares for you is very comforting and fulfilling.

Healthy relationships make our life better; they help us to carry our burdens. When you have a problem that is weighing heavily on you, having someone to talk to not only relieves the stress, but it gives you the sense that you are not carrying that burden alone. Having someone to share the burden lightens the load. Since we all suffer, healthy relationships ease our suffering.

Maintaining a shared understanding takes work. It is easy to become complacent in relationships. When we get to know someone well, we become comfortable with them. We know what to expect. We gain comfort in the idea that things are going to stay the same. However, human beings are dynamic. We are always changing. New thoughts, ideas, and experience have the potential to transform a person. Sometimes the change is gradual, but sometimes it is sudden. How we respond to change influences our relationships.

If we are committed to a shared understanding, we are open to the fact that people are always changing. Rather than see change as a threat, we see it as an opportunity for learning and growth. If you aren't open to change, you resist it. What does that look like? Constantly arguing with someone is resistance. Disagreeing with someone, but not saying anything can be resistance. Both aggressive and passive responses are signs of resistance. They both get in the way of shared understanding and healthy relationships.

Good communication skills are the most important factor in healthy relationships. They help you not only develop a shared understanding, but help you to maintain and deepen it. The goal of communication is to understand and be understood.

Understanding someone isn't the same as agreeing with them. You don't have to agree with someone in order to understand their point of view. Our natural response when someone says something we disagree with is to defend our own point of view. Our resistance (defending our point of view) is likely to create resistance in the person with whom we disagree. We can skip that step. If we first try to understand what the other person is saying, without trying to defend our own point of view, we don't create that resistance.

The more time we spend with someone, the more opportunities there are for misunderstanding. How you were raised and what you believe influence your perception of the world. You can easily misinterpret a word or phrase when you are listening to someone. Asking them what they mean promotes understanding. Defending your interpretation does not. If your goal is to understand, your actions will show it. You will ask rather than tell, and in the words of Steven Covey, author of "The Seven Habits of Highly Effective People" you will "Seek first to understand, then to be understood." The shared understanding that comes from that approach will enrich your relationships.

Exercise

Ask questions. It is not only the best way to show interest in someone, but also the best way to understand others. We all want to be understood, but if you are willing to put that desire on the back burner, and truly seek to understand another, you will build a strong foundation for your relationship.

Most people feel the need to be understood. It drives their behavior. It prompts them to say something before the other person has finished talking. It pushes them to disagree with others. It starts arguments. Make a commitment to only share your opinion when asked. When you ask a lot of questions and truly show you understand what another person is saying, they will ask your opinion; and they will listen to what you say. Because you have practiced self-control, you have positioned yourself to become a person of influence.

Insecurity

Security in a person comes from love, and insecurity from fear. Security comes from knowing who you are and what you believe. It is the awareness that you have value, and that your value lies in what you contribute to the world. Everyone has the ability to make the world better. Love is the willingness to act on that ability.

If you grew up in a loving environment, you developed a strong sense of self as part of the foundation of love you were given. That loving foundation provided you with a sense of security. You trust people. They were there for you when you needed them. They gave to you freely. Because you were given so much, you have much to give. You see relationships as an opportunity to give, not just to receive. You are aware of what you have to offer. When children receive unconditional love, they give it back freely. It is not a rare commodity. It is always there. There is no reason to save it up and ration it out sparingly. The child learns from experience that the more you give the more you get.

If a child doesn't grow up in a loving environment, this foundation may not be as solid. The security that comes from love isn't established. A child that grows up without unconditional love may not develop the same understanding of love. While it is experienced the same way, it is processed differently. It is seen as more rare, and as such, is given less freely. It is protected, coveted, and held on to. The fear of losing love becomes greater than the awareness of its true nature; that it grows only when given. When it is guarded, it becomes like water cupped in one's hand, slipping through the fingers until it disappears.

Insecure people are unaware of their capacity for love. It is as if they have a house that is sitting on a rich vein of gold, but they dig all around it, not knowing that it is right under their feet. To get to the gold, they would have to tear down the house. The gold underneath the house could build a thousand new ones, but they believe the house is all they have. They are unwilling to risk losing what they have, to gain what they could have. Insecure people become stingy with what they have in an attempt to protect it.

In contrast, people who are secure give freely. They know that what it is given freely comes back to you. Love is giving. Secure people give love because that is who they are. The love they give is a reflection of their deepest values. To overcome insecurity, people must learn to give, rather than protect, the love they have.

When love is lacking early in one's life, it can create a deep-seated insecurity that can affect relationships for a lifetime. I encouraged my children to seek relationships with people who were loved unconditionally as children; to avoid those who are selfish, or who give too much initially, only to become demanding later. While deep-seated insecurities can be overcome, it takes a great deal of compassion, patience, and energy to help someone do so effectively. When I work with people in recovery, I teach them to recognize the signs of insecurity, and seek relationships with emotionally healthy people.

It is especially challenging to avoid unhealthy relationships when you were raised in a loving environment because your natural inclination is to give. When you are a nurturing person, you tend to gravitate to where the need is the greatest. Insecure people need kindness the most. When you give love to someone who is mildly insecure, they become more secure; they give back. People that are very insecure take without giving back. Eventually, they can begin to rob you of your own security. If you don't establish boundaries and maintain them, an unhealthy relationship can make you unhealthy.

Healthy relationships are based upon reciprocity. You give, and you receive. Sometimes, one partner is more giving than the other, but over time, it balances out. Insecurity gets in the way of this because if a healthy partner is in need, the insecure partner is not focused on giving. Rather than give the healthy partner more attention because they are in need, the insecure partner demands more, or switches to "conserve" mode, to self-protect. They have difficulty seeing beyond how they feel. People who are deeply insecure have difficulty seeing beyond their own fear. This makes it difficult for an insecure person to give when their partner needs support and attention the most.

Our level of security directly impacts our relationships because it influences our actions. Insecure behavior is fearful behavior. We can overcome those fears and the habits of thinking they have created. It requires awareness. Learn to see your behavior objectively, and when you react out of fear, ask yourself, "What am I afraid of." When you do, you'll realize you are acting out of fear rather than love. Ask yourself, "What would love do?" When you decide to act out of love, you will develop the ability to give love to others while maintaining healthy boundaries.

Exercise

If you are insecure, focus on awareness of yourself and others. Do no harm. Learn to recognize how you are feeling. Communicate with those you are close to. Express your feelings with words rather than actions. Let them know how you are feeling without blame. Once you can experience fear without acting on it, you gain control and security. You can't stop the feelings, but stopping the actions will help diminish those feelings in the future. Communicating your insecurity to someone close to you reveals vulnerability. A willingness to be vulnerable is a sign of security. Doing so will make you more secure.

If you are unsure of how to act in a given situation, ask yourself, "What would love do?" Asking this simple question can guide your behavior. For example, if your significant other is going out with friends, you might feel a twinge of insecurity. Your insecure response might be to make him or her feel guilty for going out without you. When you ask, "What would love do?" the answer is likely encourage him or her to enjoy the time with friends. When you ask yourself what love would do, you remove fear from the equation.

Insecurity can arise in many different situations. If you feel insecure around people you don't know, keep this in mind. People have no idea how you feel. You could be terribly insecure, and if you don't show it, they will never know. Assume they see the best in you.

If your partner is insecure, recognize the behaviors that indicate insecurity, such as jealousy, criticism, indecisiveness, or constantly seeking validation. Do no harm. Reassure him or her of your love. Clearly communicate what you want in visible terms (what does it look like) so they have an opportunity to give you what you want. The act of giving creates more security. Also, explain what you don't want. Communicate your boundaries so they have an opportunity to learn how their behavior is affecting you. For example, you might say, "When you call me, I'd like you to ask if it's a good time to talk before you begin. Especially when I'm at work." That simple request (boundary) teaches others to be considerate of you.

When you are dealing with someone who is insecure, be patient and kind. The only person who can overcome insecurity is the person who is insecure. You can't do it for them. But you can create an environment where they are more likely to heal and grow. When people are growing and becoming more secure, they give more than they take. That is the sign of progress you should look for when evaluating how healthy the relationship is for you.

Attention

Relationships are one of the most important aspects of our lives. Attention is the currency of relationship. We have limited attention to give. Because it is limited, it is valuable. When someone tells you to pay attention, they are making a demand of your time. When you give others your attention, you are giving them something of value. In fact, your attention is the greatest thing you have to offer.

There is competition for your attention. Everyone wants it. How you spend it determines the quality of your life and your relationships. Having balance in your life means knowing what is most important to you, and giving your attention to those priorities. When you give your attention to someone or something, you are making an investment. Your actions are saying that this is important enough to give of my time and attention. Give your attention to those things that will provide a return on that investment.

A healthy body and mind must be your highest priority. If you don't give attention to the health of your body, it will take it. Ignoring what your body needs to remain healthy (good nutrition and exercise) leads to a lack of health. When you are unhealthy, your mind focuses your attention on how you feel. Have you ever tried to concentrate when you were in pain? A healthy body allows you to focus your attention elsewhere. The same goes for your mind. If you are in emotional pain, your attention is focused on that pain. It makes it difficult to think of anything or anyone else.

If you give your body and mind too much attention, it becomes unhealthy. The amount of attention you give your body should be just enough to promote health. If you spend too much attention on your body, you are taking it away from other areas of your life. For example, if you decided to start working out, and really liked the results you were getting, you might increase the amount of time you spend exercising. That time and attention has to come from somewhere. Is extra time exercising the best way to spend your time and attention? Or, could you put it into your relationships? When you put time and attention into anything to the exclusion of something more important to you, you are out of balance. People can become addicted to many things, even exercise. All addictions are a sign that your attention is out of balance.

The same applies to your mind. It is healthy to focus your attention on your thoughts and feelings so they inform your actions. Too much attention focused on them moves you out of balance. If you are focusing more on problems—than on solutions or awareness—it isn't serving you well. When your attention is focused on how you think and feel, that attention comes at the cost of something else. If you become more aware, and use that awareness to improve your actions, it is healthy. If thinking about yourself is creating a return on your investment, it is time well spent. However, if you keep thinking about a negative experience, you are reliving the experience in your mind. Negative thoughts generate negative feelings. These thoughts and feelings can hijack your attention and keep you focused inward. This is not healthy.

How much of your attention is focused inward rather than outward? Attention is energy. Energy is a source of creation and destruction. When you use it carefully, it is a creative force. Use too much of it in one area, and it becomes destructive. For example, when you think about yourself too much, you become selfish. You are taking attention and energy you should be giving to others, and using it for yourself. If you think of others too much, you can easily neglect your own wants and needs. That can lead to exhaustion and resentment. Finding balance (which is an ever moving target) is critical to your well-being.

It is in our nature to find balance. If we neglect our health, our mind will eventually bring it front and center. If we give too much attention to someone and don't receive it back, our mind responds with resentment. It is an attempt to create balance. If you resent someone, you are less likely to do something for him or her. This can bring you into balance by causing you to do less for people who don't give back. It is nature's way of maintaining balance.

There are many forces competing for our limited time and attention, and therefore our energy. In the United States, we have a consumer driven society. It began with mass media. Imagine what the world was like before it. The most important factor in people's lives was relationship. In fact, we needed each other to survive. Most people lived in rural areas. We relied upon each other to meet our needs, and we gave them most of our attention. Then came radio, followed by television. They competed with relationships for our time and attention. The better programming became, the more time and attention we gave it. Relationships take work. Listening to the radio or watching television was effortless. Since it is human nature to take the path of least resistance, we began to spend more and more time listening to the radio and watching the television, and less and less time listening and talking to each other.

Then came advertising. Its goal was to create desire. Advertisers wanted you to want what they were selling. While radio and television competed for your attention, most of the products being sold did not. Many products made life easier, and gave people more time to focus on relationships. For example, having a washing machine dramatically reduced the amount of time you had to spend doing laundry. This freed up time and attention.

In the information age, this has all changed dramatically. Many of the products being sold today compete for your attention, such as computers, cell phones, tablets, etc. Wherever you go, people are giving these devices their time and attention. To be fair, these devices are often used in relationship to people. When someone is on a social media page, they are often connecting with other people. If they are on the phone, they are talking or texting another person. These products have created more opportunities to connect with people, but these connections do not have the same quality as face-to-face communications. In addition, these products take away from current relationships. When you go to a movie theater or a restaurant, there are people with friends or family who are giving their devices their attention, rather than the people they are with. When we give most of our attention to a thing, rather than a person, we are out of balance.

Unhealthy relationships also compete for our attention. What does that look like? If someone is using any kind of force (guilt, manipulation, being overly demanding) to get your attention, it can be unhealthy. If someone has a greater need for attention, he or she may use unhealthy methods to try to get more attention from you. They are trying to take something from you. This creates resistance in you. Since they are using force, resistance to that force comes naturally. In a healthy relationship, attention is given freely.

We need relationships to stay healthy. To create value in relationships, both parties have to give of their time and attention. Attention is what makes relationships strong. It is the fuel that drives the engine. Without attention, relationships will become stagnant or die. With so many things today competing for our attention, it is difficult to spend it wisely. We have to understand the value of relationships, and how they help us to be happy. Healthy relationships help you deal with pain, and to move beyond it. They teach you about yourself. They are the mechanism with which you interact with the world. Attention is the energy that drives relationships.

Exercise

When the opportunity to give your attention to a person arises, always choose him or her over an object. Relationship has much more to offer us. If someone begins a conversation with you while you are looking at your phone, put your phone down and give him or her your full attention. Be polite. Look for every opportunity to show manners. Study etiquette. Manners are a way of communicating that we care about others. It helps us recognize all the opportunities we have to give others our attention. Make eye contact whenever you communicate with

95

someone, and communicate with someone whenever you make eye contact. Even if it is just to say hello. Because attention is one of the most valuable things we have to offer, giving it greatly influences how others perceive us.

What do you give your attention to? Make a list of what is most important to you. How much attention do you give to television? Is that on the top of the list of what's most important to you? How much attention do you give to work when you are at home? Attention is a limited resource. If you are giving it to one thing, you are taking it from another. Seek to find balance. Give your attention to those things that are most important to you.

Comfort

As an employer, I've noticed that I get the greatest effort when employees first begin the job. I don't get the best *performance* in the beginning, because they have not yet developed all of the necessary skills, but I do get the greatest effort. Anytime someone starts a new job, they feel uncomfortable. They want to do a good job. They want to succeed. They want to avoid mistakes and learn the job as quickly as they can. They want to get to the point where they feel like they know what they are doing.

Whenever we are uncomfortable, we take action to move us toward comfort. This is human nature. If you are sitting in a chair, and become uncomfortable, you shift your position to find comfort. Discomfort initiates action. Whatever the situation, if you are uncomfortable, you are motivated to move toward comfort. Discomfort is a natural, intrinsic motivator that shapes behavior.

For our ancestors, the discomfort of hunger motivated them to act. The fear of dying in winter; the fear of being shunned from their social group; and other threats to their survival created discomfort, which motivated them to action.

Threats weren't the only motivating factor. They also had a desire to create, to learn, and to grow. The creative power of the human mind is one of the greatest motivators we have once our survival needs have been met. The desire to create pushes us out of our comfort zone.

We are constantly being pulled in two directions. We want comfort, but we are happiest when we are being challenged. Challenge (discomfort) provides learning and personal growth. Most people envision a point in their lives when they will be able to take it easy. They imagine that once they get to that point, they will be happy. This isn't how it works. It is the challenges that make us stronger and it is growth that keeps us happy.

After high school, I took a job in fast food. It was my first experience with expectations that challenged me. The job provided structure that I had been lacking in my life. Around every corner was an opportunity to learn something new. I loved learning, and soon became competent and comfortable. I became bored with the job. Dissatisfaction soon followed. I waited around for management to give me new responsibilities, but they were so busy managing their own that they didn't have time to manage mine as well. That's when I realized that it was going to be "up to me" to take responsibility for my own discomfort.

I took on the tough shifts and the tough jobs that no one else wanted. I asked for the morning shift to learn how to make breakfast. By taking responsibility and challenging myself, I began to take control of my life. I saw work as someone paying me to learn; and I tried to learn all I could.

Taking on challenges that were just beyond my abilities have made all the difference in my life. I left fast food when I was recruited to work for a photo lab chain, and worked my way up to National Sales Director within that company. I continually sought greater responsibility within the company. When I had gone as far as I could, I left and started my own consulting company. A few years later, I opened my own photo lab and portrait studio, while maintaining my consulting business.

I have continually taken on new risks, and new responsibilities. I have been willing to be uncomfortable, and have used that discomfort to drive my effort. Discomfort leads to growth and learning. There is so much we would not know or learn without discomfort. Action requires motivation, and discomfort provides that motivation. So where does discomfort come from? It comes from any new situation that pushes us out of our comfort zone. We seek comfort. We want things to be easy. Without a reason to do otherwise, it is human nature to take the path of least resistance. We have to overcome that natural instinct and create our own discomfort.

Exercise

Look at comfort as a cycle. It goes from discomfort, to effort, to achievement, to satisfaction, to comfort, to dissatisfaction, to discomfort, and the cycle begins again. If you don't resist the cycle, you can actually take control of it. If you see comfort as the impetus for action, you will take action sooner if you create your own discomfort. Your effort will lead to achievement, and the achievement will lead to satisfaction and comfort. Once you recognize you are comfortable, you can create a new challenge that will create new discomfort, which will drive your actions. You are less likely to become dissatisfied if you are continually challenging yourself.

Comfort and discomfort are two sides of the same coin. Finding happiness and satisfaction is a matter of understanding how to find the balance between them. A willingness to overcome fear and push yourself outside your comfort zone will increase your happiness and satisfaction in life.

Discomfort

Discomfort not only influences your behavior, it influences everyone's behavior. It is a powerful tool that anyone can use to change their environment, but it takes a willingness to create discomfort in the process. This may seem counterintuitive. Why would you want to create discomfort? There are two primary reasons. The first is to help someone learn and grow. The second is to change someone's behavior, especially if that behavior is creating a problem for you.

Most dissatisfaction with life comes when you aren't learning and growing. The desire for comfort keeps you from taking chances. When things are easy, you don't try as hard. When I have employees who become dissatisfied with their job, it is usually because they aren't learning and growing. They have become comfortable, and aren't finding new challenges on the job.

There is a Chinese proverb that states, "The person rowing the boat doesn't have time to rock it." When an employee isn't happy, they start complaining about the job, or the customers, or their co-workers.

That is one of the first symptoms. If it continues, they will start finding problems where problems don't exist. They look for reasons for why they feel the way they do. If they are looking for a reason, they will always find one. They rarely conclude it is the result of their own choices. They usually blame someone or something else.

When employees begin acting this way, it's crucial I create opportunities for learning and growth. I have to put them in an uncomfortable situation that will motivate them to learn and grow. This usually involves giving them new responsibilities. When I do this, the first response is usually resistance. They don't want to take on any new responsibilities. They may be feeling overwhelmed by the responsibilities they already have, but it isn't the responsibilities that are weighing them down, it is how they are dealing with them. Taking on new responsibilities often requires them to delegate some of their other tasks. If some of these tasks are a source of comfort for them, they may not want to give them up. Creating discomfort, even though they resist it initially, will spur them toward productive action, and help them learn and grow.

It is the same when raising children. In the beginning, they are completely reliant on you as a parent, and they have no responsibility for their own lives. The process of raising a child to adulthood is the process of creating a human being that eventually accepts full responsibility for his or her life. It is a process. As a child becomes more capable, the parent gives the child more responsibility. Added responsibility makes the child uncomfortable. They are stuck between the desire to do it themselves, and the comfort of having it done for them.

As children get older, the more a parent does for them that they should be doing themselves, the greater the resentment that may build in that child. A parent has to be willing to create opportunities for a child to accept new responsibilities, even if the child doesn't want it. Responsibility is a learned behavior that improves with practice.

The other area where we can use discomfort to influence our environment is to use it to help someone to change. If someone is doing something that is bothering you, you want them to stop. Discomfort is a powerful tool to change behavior. If you can make someone feel uncomfortable after they demonstrate behavior you don't like, you may get them to change it. I say 'may' because another person's behavior is always their choice. Your goal is to influence the behavior, and that is the limit of your power.

A good rule of thumb is that behavior that is rewarded is likely to continue, and behavior that is punished is likely to stop. Discomfort is a subtle form of punishment. If you feel uncomfortable immediately after you do something, you are less likely to do it again. Let's say you are offended by strong language, and you have some friends that cuss regularly when talking to you. If you tell them that their language is offending you, it will make them uncomfortable. They may not acknowledge that discomfort, but telling them they have made you uncomfortable *will* make them uncomfortable. No one likes to hear that something they are doing is creating a problem for someone else. Making them feel uncomfortable every time they cuss may result in changing their behavior. They may stop cussing around you.

Creating discomfort influences behavior. But you have to be willing to feel uncomfortable yourself. It is never comfortable confronting someone's behavior. It takes a lot of courage to tell people when their behavior is affecting you negatively. Doing so makes you a stronger person, and it can raise the other person's awareness.

Silence is another discomforting tool to influence behavior. When I am interviewing candidates for a job, they have a good idea what they want to say before the interview. I use silence to get them to say more. For example, when I ask them to tell me about themselves, they give me a standard answer. When they have finished answering the question, I don't say anything. The silence makes them uncomfortable. They usually add something to what they said earlier to break the silence. When they do so, I learn more about them than I would have had I not make them feel uncomfortable.

The silence makes me feel uncomfortable as well. I want to say something to comfort the person who is obviously nervous and uncomfortable. That is our natural inclination; to comfort others when they need it. However, it sometimes works against our best interest to do so. When I interview someone for a job, I understand that the more I know, the better decision I can make. I'm willing to use discomfort to achieve my goal.

How you handle your own discomfort is very important as well. If your natural inclination is to comfort others, you may be vulnerable to manipulation. If you aren't willing to accept some discomfort, people will understand that all they have to do is make you feel uncomfortable to get what they want. They may ask for money, and you'll give it. Why? You don't want to feel uncomfortable by telling them no. They may ask you to do something you don't want to do. They may want you to agree with something you don't agree with. If you are unwilling to accept discomfort that comes with telling others no, they can easily manipulate you.

Using discomfort to shape the behavior of another person may seem manipulative. It is. You are using your behavior to influence the behavior of another. When it is defined that way, almost all interactions with others can be seen as manipulative. When you realize that all of your actions are influencing your environment, you understand the importance of choosing those actions carefully. This requires mindfulness. You must be aware of what you are doing and why you are doing it. *What* you are trying to accomplish, as well as *how* you are accomplishing it are both important. Know what you want, be willing to accept discomfort to achieve it, but do no harm in the process.

Exercise

Recognize situations that make you uncomfortable. The next time you find yourself in one of those situations, choose to stay with the discomfort rather than trying to relieve it. If silence is making you uncomfortable, do not say anything. Give it a few moments to see if the other person will act first. If someone is struggling to do something you are proficient at, give them more time to do what they are trying to do. Do not step in and do it for them. Practice patience. Do not let discomfort interfere with getting what you want.

Rewards and Behavior

Behavior that is rewarded is likely to continue. Behavior that is punished is likely to stop. This oversimplification of human behavior can be helpful in understanding people. When someone demonstrates a behavior that you don't understand, ask yourself how the person is being rewarded. If the behavior were not being rewarded, it wouldn't continue.

It is easy to see in children. When children at the grocery store want a candy bar, they ask. If the mother says no, the child may throw a tantrum. If the mother gives the child a candy bar to stop the crying, the behavior will be rewarded. If we look deeper at what is driving the behavior, it comes down to chemistry. Food releases dopamine in the brain. Dopamine is how we experience pleasure. Candy releases a lot more dopamine that broccoli. The child cries because they want a dopamine fix.

There are many things that release positive chemicals in the brain. Excitement, pleasure, attention, achievement, touch, a sense of control, and anything else we see as positive. We experience these things as positive because chemical molecules in our brains are making us feel good. If a behavior results in the release of these molecules in our brain, we perceive it as a reward, and we are likely to continue that behavior.

Imagine a mother is busy working on a project, is very involved in it, and she's ignoring her child. The child calls her and she doesn't respond. The child is seeking attention. Attention releases dopamine and gives a feeling of comfort and security.

When mother doesn't respond, children do something to get her attention. They may fall and cry, or break something, or get between their mother and whatever task she is giving her attention to. This may result in their mother getting angry, and punishing them. The behavior is still being rewarded. How? She is giving them attention. When a child is looking for attention, even negative attention is better than none.

We don't change that much when we become adults. We continue to seek attention. If our need for attention goes frequently unmet during our childhood, we often continue to seek a disproportionate amount as an adult. A look at some common stereotypes will illustrate this point. A woman who dresses in revealing clothes may be looking for… attention. A man who drives a sports car may be looking for… attention. A man or woman that causes a "scene" at a restaurant may be looking for… attention. Attention is the currency of relationships. It releases dopamine. It gives us a sense of security and comfort. We seek it. We are social beings because we are rewarded for being social. It is how our brains are wired.

When you look at behavior as actions that create a dopamine release in the brain, you can use that information to not only understand behavior (both yours and others), you can use it to shape behavior as well. Why does someone criticize you or put you down, or argue with you constantly? Feeling superior to others releases dopamine in the brain. Why does someone stay in an unhealthy relationship? Attention (even negative attention) releases dopamine in the brain. If someone's negative behavior releases dopamine into the brain, the best way to shape that behavior is to remove the reward. If someone criticizes you, let them know how the behavior has affected you. By making them aware that they have caused harm, it takes away the dopamine. Your goal isn't to make them feel bad, it is simply to make them aware of the consequences of their actions. Awareness of negative consequences short-circuits the dopamine response. If the behavior isn't rewarded, it is less likely to continue.

This general rule doesn't apply when dealing with addiction. When someone is addicted to a drug, the release of dopamine is so great, that you will not be able to shape behavior this way. The need for the dopamine becomes so important that the individual will do almost anything, and forsake any relationship, to get their fix. This is why threats and reason don't work with addicts. The need for dopamine hijacks their brain to the extent that the small amount they may get through relationship pales in comparison. The more extreme the personality or situation you are working with, the less power you have to influence their behavior.

Exercise

When you experience a situation that you don't understand, ask yourself how the behavior is being rewarded. What is happening that is causing the release of dopamine? Is it happening because he or she is receiving attention? Is it because a belief is being validated? Whatever the reason, teaching yourself to be aware of the underlying motivations can help you positively influence the situation if that is your goal. If that isn't your goal, it will at least help you see the situation clearer. Understanding releases dopamine as well.

Ask for what you want

How do you want other people to treat you? We all have an idea of how we would like to be treated, but have you ever defined it? Every relationship has expectations. With closer, more intimate relationships, such as friends and family, we have greater expectations. Once someone gets to know us, we assume he or she knows what we want. We judge the quality of the relationship on the other's ability to anticipate and meet our needs.

Much of the pain in relationships comes from what people do, but a lot comes from what they don't do. When someone does something you don't like, you confront the behavior. Doing so reduces the likelihood of it happening again. By acting after the fact, you have influenced future behavior. This works very well when identifying what you "don't want." Someone's behavior triggers a negative response in you, you confront it by letting the other person know how their behavior has affected you, and hopefully the person will stop doing it.

How do we respond when something we want to happen doesn't happen? The key is good communication. It is a bit more difficult to identify what we want than what we don't want. When someone does something that we don't like, we know right away. When someone doesn't do something we want them to do, we don't recognize it as quickly because it doesn't trigger a negative emotional response. We may know something is missing, but aren't quite sure what it is.

The first step in knowing what you want is to become aware of your expectations. These are often triggered by disappointment. When you are disappointed, it means your expectations weren't met. When we are disappointed, we usually blame someone else. Blame is the opposite of responsibility. We must overcome the natural inclination to blame others for our disappointment and identify the role we have played in the situation. Blame interferes with awareness.

The second step is to define what we want to happen looks like, and how it was different from what did happen. If you can't describe what you want in visible terms, how can you communicate that expectation to someone else? You must be able to say, "Here's what I want and here's what it looks like."

The third step is to ask for what you want. Timing is very important. If asking triggers a negative response or other resistance, it's an indication that the timing may be off. The goal is to make the other person aware of what you want. If they respond defensively, decide to discuss it later. You aren't trying to control him or her. You are simply trying to raise his or her awareness of what you want. If they become defensive again when you try to discuss it, it's an indication that it is a topic they don't want to discuss. If it is important to you, it's worth discussing.   Insist on discussing it and communicate through the resistance. Don't let the other person make you feel so uncomfortable that you give up communicating what you want.

Let's take a typical example. Tom and Carol have been married for three years. They both get home from work around five. On Wednesday, it's Carol's turn to cook dinner, so she starts it soon after getting home. Tom gets home, gives Carol a hug and a kiss hello, turns on the television and sits in his recliner while Carol prepares dinner. Carol has had a busy day, and there is a lot she'd like to talk to Tom about. She talks to him while she cooks, but he's paying more attention to the television than to her. She's disappointed when Tom doesn't respond to what she's saying.

In this situation, Carol will usually respond in one of two ways. She will feel the disappointment, but won't say anything to Tom. He may sense her anger as they both sit down to eat, but won't have any idea where it is coming from. When Carol gets to work the next day, her friends and co-workers will hear all about it, but Tom doesn't have a clue.

Or, Carol may choose to respond to her disappointment right away by confronting Tom. She may say she is tired of him ignoring her, and accuse him of never helping out when it is her turn to cook dinner. Tom will become irritated, because she is interrupting the television program he is watching. He may get up and ask her what's wrong, while leaving the television blaring in the background. It may escalate into an argument, or they may decide not to argue, but to state their position and go back to what they were doing. Tom may say that they agreed to share the cooking, and it is his night off. He should be able to relax while

Carol is cooking. He may say that he doesn't ask for Carol's help when *he* is cooking dinner.

Let's take a look at what Carol really wants. After a long day at work, she wants to talk with Tom about how her day went. She has been away from him all day, and she wants to share with him the experiences she has had while they were apart. And she wants his full attention while she does so.

What does Tom want? After a long day at work, he doesn't want to talk about it. He likely doesn't even want to think about it. He wants to sit in front of the television and be mindless for a while. This helps him to get rid of the stress. Men reduce stress by engaging in mindless behavior for a while. Women reduce stress by talking about it.

What does Carol want? How and when should she ask for it? Carol wants to talk to Tom about her day when she gets home, and she wants his full attention. What would that look like? When Tom got home, he would immediately greet Carol and would not turn on the television. He might ask her what she would like him to do to help with dinner, and would do it while he listened to her talk about her day. Tom would give Carol his full attention while they prepared dinner together, and that attention would continue while they ate. After dinner, Carol would clean up while Tom turned on the television and sat in his recliner. Carol would join him when she was finished, but would either watch television with him, or would read a magazine, or both, but wouldn't start any conversation, because it was time for Tom to de-stress.

This would meet Carol's need to communicate and to receive attention, and Tom's need to "be mindless" without any distractions.

Now that we know what Carol wants, how and when does she ask for it? The best time to ask is before expectations have been established for the day. I would suggest a discussion in the morning before they both go to work. If Carol brings it up right when Tom gets home, she is already interfering with his expectations. He expected to get home and sit in front of the television and relax while Carol cooked dinner. If she brings it up after work, she is competing with his expectations. If she brings it up in the morning, she is helping to shape his expectations.

Carol could begin by saying, "Tom, I'd like to ask you if you'd be willing to do something for me tonight. I feel like we've been in a bit of a rut, and I'd like us to change what we do after work. After a long day at work, it is very helpful if I can talk with you. We've been apart all day, and I want to share with you what I did while we were apart. I understand that you telling me about your day isn't as important to you, and that you'd rather chill in front of the television, but it is very important to me. Would you be willing to try something a little different?" Tom might ask, "What did you have in mind?"

Carol would respond by saying, "When you get home from work, I'd like you to wait a while before you turn on the television. If you would give me your full attention while I cook dinner, you could even cook it with me, and after dinner, I would do the clean up while you watch tv. I know you need to relax, but if you could wait an hour to do it, it would make me much happier. I know you don't need to talk about your day, but I do. Would you be willing to try it tonight?" If he agrees, she could also call him late in the afternoon while he is still at work and remind him she is looking forward to talking with him when he gets home. This will remind him if he forgot.

Many things interfere with what we want. One of the things that gets in the way of a shared understanding is judgment. If you believe he *should* know what you want, you are judging. If you don't ask for what you want, and don't remind him when he isn't doing it, how can you judge? Judging is a form of blame. If it's the other person's fault, it's not yours.

When people say relationships take work, this is what they are talking about. It takes effort to communicate what you want. Why don't we do it? It is easier to blame the other person, rather than take responsibility for what we are getting. Another reason people are hesitant to ask for what they want is that they are worried about not getting it, and what that would mean. If you tell someone what you want, and that person is unwilling to give it, it may cause you pain.

Sometimes it takes us a while to understand what we really want in our relationships. Once we know, we have a responsibility to let others know. It not only makes our life better, but has the potential to make others' lives better as well; communicating what we want makes others more aware. When they see that their actions are making your life better, they are becoming a more aware person in the process. We learn by what we do. Sometimes, if someone we love tells us what they want, it guides our actions and makes us more aware. We have a responsibility to share not only what we have, but also what we want, with the world. Not to be selfish, but to help make the world a better place by making ourselves, and the people in it more aware.

Exercise

Think about your most important relationships. Ask yourself what you would like those relationships to look like. Pick one of them; it can be a friend, a spouse or partner, a parent, or a child. Write down what you would like them to do that they aren't currently doing. Then write down something you would like them to stop doing. If they are doing something that is bothering you, make a commitment to discuss it when the time is right. If they aren't doing something you want them to do, discuss that as well. Be prepared to describe the behavior in visible terms.

Explain why you want them to start doing something, or stop doing something. Address the behavior in terms of how it affects you. Don't try to assign motives, as that may start an argument. Rather than say, "Why are you trying to punish me with the silent treatment?" say something like, "When you don't talk to me, I feel like I've done something wrong and I don't have any idea what it is."

Your goal is to communicate what you want. Don't make the other person guess. Put it out there! Let them know what your expectations are. They may or may not be able to meet those expectations, but if you communicate them clearly, you'll have a better chance of getting what you want.

Good and Bad

Most people like chocolate. Imagine eating only chocolate for breakfast, lunch and dinner. You would get sick of it. What makes chocolate so good, is not having chocolate. Its value comes from its absence. Most aspects of life reflect this idea. Life has value because of death. Wealth has value because of poverty. Plenty has value because of scarcity. Happiness has value because of sadness. Without the bad, there would not be the good. It is the bad times that make the good times even better. It is difficult to see when we are in difficult situations, but it is part of the cycle and balance of life.

If everything were easy, you would have little appreciation for what you have. Not having, is what makes having, so good. When you work hard to earn something, what you get is not only the thing you worked for, but also a sense of value that comes from knowing how hard you worked to get it.

Our expectations have a great deal to do with our dissatisfaction. The term "happily ever after" implies that there will be no sadness. But sadness will always be part of the deal. If we understand and expect it, we are much better prepared to deal with it when it happens. Looking back on my life, I am grateful for the difficult times. They not only have made me who I am, they have given me an appreciation for the good times. Without the bad, how would we recognize the good?

Every life has good and bad. The fact that they are occurring means you are alive. That you are alive is the greatest fact in the universe! Without that, nothing else would matter. There are days you feel low when you get up. There are days you feel great. Moods come and go. It is part of who we are. Challenges come and go. Everything you survive prepares you to take on greater challenges.

And life will present greater challenges. We don't hit a point where life becomes easy and everything will always be good. Life gets more and more difficult, but you become more and more capable. It is the difficulties in life that make you a more capable person; a person more capable of making the world a better place. If you hadn't experienced a mean person, would you understand the value of kindness? If you had never lost someone you loved, would you understand the preciousness of time? It is through our suffering that we learn how to live.

If you focus on the pain, rather than see it as part of the process, fear will take more and more of your attention. It will take that attention away from you, and from everyone else you could be giving it to. Fear should inform our actions, not dictate them. If we can take our attention away from how bad we are feeling, and focus it on what the pain has taught us, we move forward in love, rather than shrink in fear.

Exercise

See pain as a teacher, and all difficulty as a lesson you need to learn. The value in this approach is that it shapes your thinking. It takes your experience and forges it into a tool with which you can build a better life. Focusing on pain makes you a victim. Focusing on what the pain is teaching you makes you wise.

Nothing ever lasts. Tough times will pass, as will the good times. Learn to stay fully aware when both occur. When you appreciate the good times, it allows you to savor their richness longer. When you suffer through bad times, find comfort in the realization that it will get better. Loss can teach us to appreciate what we have. Find things to be grateful for and focus on them daily. Just saying a prayer of thanks every day can help you to lead a happier life. If you are alive, there is much to be thankful for.

Love and Reciprocity

There are many kinds of loving action. Some require little effort, others greater effort. Kindness, respect, compassion, patience, and consideration are all small efforts we can make with everyone, every day. More important relationships require a greater investment. We invest more by giving our attention and affection.

In our most important relationships, we not only give, but we share. We share our burdens as well as our joy. We not only share our happiness, but our doubts, insecurities, and fear. We do this not to burden others, but to help others understand who we are. We trust that they will not only share our burdens, but will also share their burdens with us. This is intimacy. It is the ability to trust another with good and bad, joy and sorrow, love and pain.

In relationship, we give and we receive. Reciprocity is the basis of all healthy relationships. If we give without receiving anything back, we begin to resent others. If we receive without giving back to others, they begin to resent us. Love gives. When we love others, we want to give them all we have to offer. Anything that we can give to make another's life better, we freely give it. We are happy to give, and grateful when we receive. In a perfect world, there would never be negative consequences of loving action. Our intention would determine our outcome. However, this isn't always the case.

With love comes responsibility. We must see beyond how we feel, and understand the consequences of our actions: even loving actions. Because we don't live in a perfect world, we must invest our love wisely. Because small investments like kindness and compassion require so little, but have such a great return, we should make them everywhere. Where our investment is greater (our time and attention), we must be more selective. Our time and attention are the greatest rewards we have to offer. We must be wise with whom we choose to share them. Our greatest investments should be reserved for healthy relationships that promise the greatest return.

I've worked with many women who have been in abusive relationships. They learned that if you give to someone who does not give back, you are teaching him it is okay to receive without giving. Allowing others to take without giving does harm. Some entered into abusive relationships because they didn't feel they deserved better. One way in which they began to understand their worthiness was by asking them if their child deserved to have a loving relationship when he or she got older. If so, how could they deserve any less? They had to learn to see themselves through the eyes of a loving parent, even if they didn't have one. To love oneself is to become worthy of receiving the love of another. We all deserve love. Part of keeping our relationships healthy is in finding a balance between giving and receiving.

Exercise

We all have a responsibility to create balance in our relationships. If you are in a relationship that is unbalanced, identify what you are doing that is contributing to that imbalance. Don't expect others to know what you want and then resent them when they don't do it. If you aren't getting what you want, ask for it. Give, and expect to receive. If you don't receive, ask for what you want. If you don't get it, perhaps it's time to evaluate the relationship.

If you are in a relationship in which you receive much more than you give, look for ways to give in order to balance it out. If you don't, he or she may become resentful. If they want to give more than you can reciprocate, find ways to limit what they can do for you. Sometimes people overstep boundaries when giving. It is up to you to enforce those boundaries to protect yourself. Sometimes people give in order to create an obligation. This is manipulative and harmful. They can only succeed if you allow them to violate your boundaries. Communicate your boundaries. Asserting yourself takes a willingness to be uncomfortable. Accepting a little discomfort dramatically increases your ability to influence your environment.

Forgiveness

When I went to church as a child, I learned about forgiveness. The idea was closely linked to the idea of "do unto others." Forgiveness was something I did for someone else. The idea went like this. Someone did something that hurt you. They apologized; you forgave them so they didn't continue to feel bad for what they did. That made you a better person. That was the end of it.

While forgiveness may help the person who has hurt you, have you ever considered how it helps you? When someone does something that hurts you, you experience pain. It may be physical pain, emotional pain, or both. You create a strong memory of the experience. Every time you think about it, you experience the pain again. Forgiveness is the conscious decision to let go of the pain.

Fear influences your behavior. If you haven't forgiven, when you interact with them again, fear drives your actions rather than love. You may treat them with disrespect or some other unkind act. That they hurt you is a fact. However, that is in the past. What is driving your behavior now is not what they are doing, but your memory of what they did. Your memory is now a thought. That thought is driving your behavior.

What we choose to give our time and attention (energy) to becomes stronger. When we think about the memory of the pain, our fear increases. The stronger the fear, the greater influence it will have on our behavior. Eventually, this fear will control us. We want to be kind, but whenever we interact with this person, we are mean. Simply put, the memory of this person's action is controlling our behavior. When we refuse to forgive, we are choosing to allow another person's act to continue to negatively influence our behavior. We are giving a person who has hurt us continued power over our life! Their action (which hurt us) was their choice. We can't change what happened. However, by refusing to forgive, we are making a commitment to continue the pain indefinitely!

Forgiveness is the decision to stop giving energy (thought and attention) to the memory of what happened. There is no need to forget. Just stop thinking about it. Put your energy into how you want to be. When you choose to think of something else, you take away the power of the memory. When you consciously choose how you will interact with the person, you act with intention, rather than react with fear. It doesn't mean you have to tolerate any more hurt from them. You simply be the person you want to be, regardless of what they do or did. If they say or do something that is hurtful, you can simply say, "What you just said/did hurt me. I don't want to be around you right now. Goodbye." Then leave.

There is no need to be unkind. Be who you want to be. Don't give the other person power over your response. Don't let the memory of what they have done in the past control who you are in the present. Forgiveness is for you. It is a gift you give yourself. It is the decision to reallocate your energy. It is the choice to stop giving energy to the memory of your pain.

Exercise

Learn to forgive people in advance. All of the pain we have suffered in our lives has created memories. Those memories influence our actions. We can become defensive in order to protect ourselves from potential hurt feelings. Defensive actions we take can create defensive reactions in others. If you are a friendly person, and you are taken advantage of, you may become an unfriendly person to protect yourself. If you do this, you have chosen to give the people who have harmed you in the past control over who you are in the present. These people are the ones who should have the least amount of influence over who you are. When you choose to forgive people in advance, it means that you will not let their pain continue in you. You are making a conscious decision to say the pain stops right here, right now, with me.

ABOUT THE AUTHOR

Randy Large is the President of the Consulting Consortium, Inc. and the Owner/Managing Partner of Sherrie's Studio. He lives in Farmington, New Mexico.

Contact Information:

Randy Large

Consulting Consortium, Inc

PO Box 6311

Farmington, NM 87499

randy@randylarge.com

www.randylarge.com